The School Leadership Juggle

The School Leadership Juggle

Balancing Primary School Education While Navigating Real-World Challenges

Andrew Oberthur

Praise for *The School Leadership Juggle*

There are plenty of voices these days telling principals how to do their work. Part of the problem is they come from those who have never done it. Andrew Oberthur is definitely not one of these. Years of practice, deep reflection, and commitment to the joy of leading communities of learning energises his writing. It's not starry-eyed, though, and he broaches the challenges and rewards of school leadership. Find a comfy chair ... you'll enjoy the read.

Dr Paul Kidson
Senior Lecturer in Educational Leadership
Australian Catholic University

Andrew paints a realistic picture of the scope and challenges for school-based leadership teams. At the same he offers clear sound advice and direction for those who are, or aspiring to be, leaders.

Phil McGreevy
Staff Instructional Coach

I found reading this book very useful in better understanding the work undertaken by school leadership and teachers. I would recommend this book to all those seeking a deeper understanding of how a school operates, the challenges facing school leadership and teachers and potential solutions for those challenges.

Alanna Bolger
Parent

Andrew has given us an unflinching look at the challenges faced by teachers and school leaders in today's educational system. He states the obvious: 'The current model is NOT realistic and NOT sustainable' and he offers honest, practical solutions for each challenge. While some of these solutions can only be provided by outside authorities (for example, funding to hire more teachers and other personnel and raising teacher pay), other solutions are within the control of school leaders. Andrew asks the tough questions and doesn't shy away from offering bold solutions. We need more books like this one!

Willy Wood
Educational Consultant, USA

Published by Amba Press
Melbourne, Australia
www.ambapress.com.au

Editor: Francesca Hoban Ryan
Cover designer: Tess McCabe

ISBN: 9781923116252 (pbk)
ISBN: 9781923116269 (ebk)

A catalogue record for this book is available from the National Library of Australia.

Contents

Foreword

In today's ever-changing educational landscape, school leaders and teachers face increasingly complex and demanding responsibilities. Balancing the core business of education with the multitude of challenges that arise in their day-to-day work can be an overwhelming task. It is within this context that Andrew Oberthur's *The School Leadership Juggle* emerges as a valuable resource for leaders and teachers seeking guidance, support and strategies to navigate the intricate juggling act that is their profession.

Drawing from his extensive experience as an educator, administrator and researcher, Oberthur provides a comprehensive exploration of the multifaceted world of primary school education. The book delves into various responsibilities such as curriculum design, classroom management, student assessment, parent engagement and professional development, highlighting the need for principals to adeptly manage these tasks while fostering student success and maintaining their passion for teaching.

What distinguishes *The School Leadership Juggle* is its practical approach. Oberthur acknowledges that school leaders and staff require more than abstract theories; they need tangible tools and strategies to excel in their roles. The book offers evidence-based techniques, tips and insights that educators can readily implement in their daily practice. Whether new or experienced, readers will find a wealth of practical wisdom to enhance their effectiveness.

Furthermore, the book acknowledges the emotional toll of juggling multiple responsibilities. Teaching is a calling driven by a genuine desire to make a positive impact on young minds. However, the demands and expectations placed on school leaders and educators can lead to burnout and stress. *The*

School Leadership Juggle compassionately addresses this aspect, reminding school staff to prioritise self-care, establish boundaries and seek support when needed. By addressing the emotional dimension, Oberthur equips educators with the resilience necessary to thrive in their profession.

Another strength of the book lies in its emphasis on collaboration. Oberthur recognises that education is a shared endeavour, and fostering strong relationships and partnerships with colleagues, parents and the community is vital. Collaboration allows educators to share the workload, learn from each other and create a supportive network. Throughout the book, practical strategies for building collaborative environments and nurturing these relationships are provided.

In conclusion, *The School Leadership Juggle* is an indispensable guide for primary school leaders and teachers. Andrew Oberthur's expertise and passion for education shine through, making this book a valuable resource for educators at all stages of their careers. By offering practical strategies and addressing the emotional aspects of the profession, the book empowers educators to thrive in their juggling act. It encourages readers to approach it with an open mind and embrace new perspectives, allowing the wisdom within its pages to ignite their passion, inspire their practice and make a lasting impact on the lives of their students.

Dr Michael Stewart
Principal and Author

Introduction

Is it possible for primary school principals to be leaders of learning while they have ultimate responsibility for many other school issues? While education authorities expect principals to be leaders of learning, and principals share the same ambition, a vast array of other responsibilities often occupy the majority of their time.

Is it possible for teachers to be brilliant and fulfil the incredibly high expectations placed on them by education authorities, their school communities and wider society while maintaining their own personal health, wellbeing and family life? Most teachers find teaching a great joy most of the time, yet there is substantial evidence that the profession is becoming less attractive and less sustainable due to the increasing demands and pressures placed on educators.

This book will unpack the various and complex responsibilities of primary school principals and aspiring school leaders, and offer strategies to assist them in juggling the core business of their work.

The principal is responsible for leading a school (Queensland Department of Education, 2023). They are primarily involved in educational leadership and the overall management of all school staff, contributing to the establishment and maintenance of a supportive school environment and learning culture. School leaders must be involved in leading the learning direction and creating the learning culture of their school. They have oversight of the policies and vision of the school, setting the direction with the relevant stakeholders to move forward into a better place. The improved academic performance of the students is often used as one measure of success of a school leader, along with the development of a positive school culture and improved facilities. Once a principal finishes at a school, their legacy may be measured against these broad criteria.

Teachers are responsible for the teaching and learning process. Their performance may be measured against the academic improvement and standards of their students.

Education is so much more than academic performance, positive school culture and improved facilities. This book will explore the myriad of responsibilities and duties in primary schools and discuss how school principals and aspiring leaders can not only fulfil but exceed expectations in their roles.

Staff instructional coach Phillip McGreevy describes the change in education in recent years:

> like a juggler or a juggling troupe – keeping as many various sized props in the air before they are dropped. This is similar to what's happening for principals and school leaders as they attempt to juggle their core business with the plethora of reality demands. The problem is the number and size of the demands keeps increasing.

Currently there appears to be little inspiration for school leaders to remain in their job and strive for excellence. It is demoralising for some. Much of a principal's time is devoted to discretionary activities that do not have a directly measurable impact on teaching and learning.

Numerous tasks that principals undertake may be considered discretionary activities not mandatory to the core business of teaching and learning. This book will unpack some of these discretionary activities and align them with the mandatory activities that impact the teaching and learning process. We will also explore the amount of autonomy and choice that principals have, or don't have, in determining where they could and should be investing their time as school leaders. See Appendix Three for an example of a principal's email folder list and notice how much is linked to teaching and learning or students.

Teachers, and aspiring leaders too, are often asked to undertake numerous roles that have minimal impact on the teaching and learning process. How and why they juggle their core business with the numerous other time-occupying activities will be explored. As retired teacher Oliver Scodellaro reflected:

If a child doesn't know how to ride a bike, then schools are expected to teach bike skills. If a child can't manage their money, schools are expected to teach financial literacy. If a child is using social media, then the school is expected to teach safe internet usage. It's impossible to teach EVERYTHING. Schools are there to teach children how to think.

If you follow the news, you will encounter numerous headlines that indicate challenges for principals and teachers. The impact of the juggle appears to be harming principals, teachers and ultimately our students.

'Number of principals planning to quit or retire triples since 2019'

'Are Australian schools facing a principal crisis?'

'Australian teachers plan to quit'

'Principals at breaking point'

'New help for schools as teacher shortage bites'

'Public school principals fighting with one hand tied behind their backs'

'Teacher burnout hits record'

'Teachers are not to blame for their own burnout'

'Queensland education staff quitting in record numbers'

'Revealed: 350 schools struggling with teacher shortages'

'$200K reasons why teachers are leaving their job'

'Top heavy – centralised school system failing students'

'Teachers quitting in droves'

'Principal profession facing perfect storm, expert warns'

'Workloads Slashed for NSW Teachers'

'60-hour weeks and sleepless nights – Why Australia's principals are leaving in droves.'

'Program combats 'lonely at the top' mentality for principals'

'How resilience can help principals bounce back from burnout'

Education authorities should be alarmed by these headlines. They must find ways to attract and retain high-quality teachers and school leaders. Failing to do this will have a detrimental effect on the educational standards in Australia, which are already below where we would like them to be.

Many of the discretionary activities at schools are wonderful community-building exercises and create a culture of trust and collaboration amongst the community stakeholders. School fetes, concerts, assemblies and carnivals all bring the community together and often showcase the students' talents. The impact on teaching and learning may be minimal, yet the value of these activities can be enormous in creating a positive school culture and community. The time and energy they take to plan and execute can also be immense. Every activity also detracts from the time and energy that teachers and leaders need to teach and learn.

This book will refer to educators, representing teachers and school leaders. On occasions the text will refer to school leaders, representing principals and deputies. If teachers are discussed, then the topic will be unique to them. As most principals start out as teachers, they should have an understanding of the complexities of the role.

The current model is NOT realistic and NOT sustainable. We need change and we need it now! This book aims to give principals and aspiring leaders some practical strategies to manage the official core business with the reality. While juggling can be fun, it can also be draining and demoralising.

This book aims to give hope while challenging the status quo.

Let's engage in optimistic dialogue, let's take control of our professional lives, do our job to best of our abilities and remind the education authorities that wellbeing conditions can be created to give us a sustainable workforce, making a positive difference in the lives of our students. After all, the students are the reason we do what we do.

1

Focusing on the Core Business of Education

Most school leaders started their careers in education as fresh-faced young teachers or latecomers wanting to make a difference in the lives of young people. As their careers evolve and opportunities arise, some teachers move into leadership positions. Others may redirect to specialisations, remain as classroom practitioners or leave the profession. I identified these trends after attending my 35-year teacher college reunion!

Teachers want to see students learn new skills, concepts, processes, content and ways to learn so they can be set up for future study, jobs and contribute to the world that they will create (Barrett, 2017).

Primary school teachers are the second, possibly third educators in line to influence children's development. Parents are the first educators, followed by the early childhood educators, before the children enter primary school and begin the formal process of learning in mainstream classrooms (for the majority of children, with home schooling and alternative education provisions gaining a little traction in recent years, largely influenced by the opportunities afforded some parents during the global pandemic). Children spend most of their waking hours with primary school teachers and the impact of their teachers cannot be understated..

As teachers transition into leadership roles, their motivation to explore leadership may continue on the same trajectory, as their desire to have a positive influence on more students is a key rationale for becoming a school leader (KU Online Education Graduate Programs Blog, 2023). Principals have the capacity to influence the teaching and learning outcomes of students by leading the school's direction and guiding the teaching and auxiliary staff, all of whom influence students' development. International research reports that successful principals demonstrate "a strong values orientation relating to clear instrumental and broad moral purposes, along with other similar attributes, qualities, and strategies, recur as common denominators" (Day, 2007). There is some correlation between what motivates educators to be principals and what it means for leaders, in their sense of purpose.

The principal develops a vision for the school, based on a clear moral purpose and commitment to the learning and growth of young people and adults (AITSL, 2014). Principals are instructional leaders who ensure students receive teaching of the highest quality and a range of learning opportunities in order to reach their potential (Queensland Department of Education, 2023). It is the responsibility of the school principal and the leadership team to ensure that staff have adequate resources and time to meet the standards. This means the principal and a leadership team must be able to provide feedback for the teachers, professional development for the teachers and the facilities and the resources for all children to access the curriculum and continue to progress in their learning journey. Unfortunately, there may be competing priorities for the school leadership team to manage and to direct.

This chapter is going to unpack the core responsibilities of the leadership team in relation to the teaching-learning process, while identifying some of the competing priorities which may in fact distract them from their core business on occasions.

Learning and Teaching Process

If we analyse the teaching-learning process from the start of the year through to the end of the year, we can identify the elements associated with providing high-quality teaching and learning and what it means for teachers and school leaders to prepare to meet the needs of all their learners. So, let's start with planning and preparation.

Planning and Preparation

All teachers need time to read and understand the curriculum. Teachers need time to collaborate with their colleagues efficiently so that they can plan lessons that will meet the needs of individual learners. They need to be able to access resources, find materials, plan lessons and ensure there is a learning sequence that will cover the curriculum and provide engaging enriching opportunities for all students. The school leaders have a role to play in this by providing the time, space and resources. They must support the staff in modelling good practices, in continuing their professional learning along with the staff. As pedagogical changes occur, the way we accommodate diverse learning changes too. School principals should continue to learn while guiding and modelling the teaching process, indicating to teachers that school leaders are also involved in the learning journey.

Leaders have an important role to play because they set the direction for the school; let me give you an example. There is an age-old debate about the place of textbooks in schools. Some leaders would be advocates for textbooks in schools while others say textbooks won't be used in their school. This then is a philosophical debate around pedagogy and around how teachers should or should not, could or could not be teaching and instructing their students. That is just one example of how leaders could and should do it. Similarly, where school leader chooses to invest their time, energy, money in particular curriculum and co-curricular activities.

As teachers move on from planning, now comes the exciting part of education: teaching and working with students. This is the reason why many teachers get into teaching, to make a positive influence on the lives of young students. Teachers need to know their students and how they learn. To achieve this, teachers may do some 'get to know you' activities early in the school year or have students complete some pre-tests, particularly in the essentials of literacy and numeracy. Teachers may give the students a profile questionnaire for them to complete, which could explore the student's interests, learning style, motivational triggers – anything that may assist the teacher to understand the individual students and the class as a collective. Students bring prior knowledge to class every day. Each new year builds on the skills and knowledge learned in the preceding years. When John Hattie (2011) says 'know thy learner', he is stressing that teachers need to know their students' current abilities, their prior and current knowledge and how they learn. Teachers, in most cases, have access to previous years' records of student results. Schools keep copies of previous report cards, hard copy or electronic, which teachers may read to understand their learners. While it is important that teachers welcome each cohort of learners without any preconceived ideas about the students, it is also advantageous to have relevant knowledge of their learners so there are no surprises. To be forewarned is to be forearmed.

Schools may also adopt the practice of giving the teachers a class profile, which gives them a snapshot of their class. At an immediate glance, teachers can see the general ability of their class, with the profile including data about literacy, numeracy, behaviour, special needs, and possibly comments about their family, if relevant. It would be preferable that this data be visible electronically, however until such a system is available and personalised for each school or class, a paper copy will have to suffice. The advantage of this profile is that the data is provided by the teachers who most recently taught that student. School leaders are encouraged to put the class lists together at the end of the year and before the teachers finish the year, they complete this 'tick and flick' profile, with the knowledge of their students. This then creates the most current profile of the class for next year's teacher. Very handy! Note: these profiles can also be used when principals have to assign students to a class, if they commence mid-year. A check on the class profile can allow an informed decision to be made as to where an incoming child should best be placed, if the school leaders choose multiple criteria beyond purely class size and gender balance. These criteria should be considered along with the academic and behaviour profile of a class.

Teaching

Teachers are responsible for implementing the curriculum, providing engaging, exciting learning opportunities for their students and ensuring that the needs of the diverse learners in their classrooms will be met. Now you may be wondering how does the school leader influence what happens in the classroom? There are schools and systems of schools that would have expectations on the pedagogy that is practised. For example, some systems of schools may have effective and expected practices which they anticipate all teachers will embed in their daily practice. According to Sharratt and Fullan (2012) these high yield strategies include the use of learning intentions and success criteria, regular feedback to students, whole part whole teaching strategy and the 4Cs model of pedagogy (co-construct, co-plan, co-teach and co-review). The use of learning intentions and success criteria, as described by some educational leaders, would be considered an expected and effective practice to ensure the learners know what and why they are learning a specific lesson. Teachers providing feedback would also be an expected practice that would encourage growth in students' learning. Learning walks and talks, or walk-throughs, are also another high yield strategy that teachers may be expected to use. The school leaders enter classrooms, during lessons, and ask the individual students a number of directed questions which then gives the leadership team feedback as to the effectiveness of the pedagogy that is being used. These strategies are proven to have a positive impact on learning outcomes for all students. As such it is the principal's responsibility to make sure the teachers meet those pedagogical expectations.

I just mentioned the important questions that leaders may ask students when visiting classrooms. These questions are:

- What are you learning?
- How are you going?
- How do you know?
- How can you improve?
- Where do you go for help?

As you can see school leaders have an important role to play to direct the pedagogy that is expected to be used in classrooms. The pedagogy teachers should be using is research-based, evidence-based so that we understand what we're doing. High-quality pedagogy and teaching practices will have significant impact on student outcomes.

Now as part of the planning process it is imperative that the teachers know and understand the curriculum. They should be able to identify the line-of-sight documents and the achievements standards that they are using to guide their plan and their pedagogy. They should be able to use and analyse monitoring tools and the data those monitoring tools create to also guide their planning and their teaching around those core literacy and numeracy priorities.

Pedagogy

Once again, we have to ask: how might, or how should, or how does the school leadership team influence the pedagogy in the classroom? School leaders ask the teachers to embed certain high yield strategies, effective and expected practices to ensure high-quality teaching and learning for all learners. Pedagogical approaches may include the whole part whole strategy. Another strategy is the inquiry approach to learning, where a question is a catalyst for exploring answers. The strategy of 'I do, we do, you do' is also another effective strategy. Being an instructional leader means the principal can give the teachers the guidance necessary to adopt and adapt such strategies for their class.

Teachers must know their subject area, be it in primary school or high school. Primary school generalist teachers must know all the subject areas that they are responsible for teaching. Some knowledge of the curriculum will come about through pre-service courses in undergraduate degrees. It also come about through ongoing professional learning that the leadership team will provide for their teachers throughout the year. And as the curriculum evolves, professional learning will be necessary to keep abreast of latest trends in education. As pedagogy evolves teachers may need to attend professional learning or have practices modelled to them so they can implement research-based practices that have most impact on students' learning. Again, the school leaders are responsible for driving this direction so that they can be confident that their teachers have all the knowledge and opportunity to learn and implement high-quality practices in their classrooms.

The next step in the teaching-learning cycle will be the assessment that students will undergo to indicate their progress in a particular subject or subjects. So as part of the planning process teachers may begin with the end in mind. They should be asking themselves **where are the students at and where do I want to get them to?** This may take the form of doing some pre-testing at the start of a unit so that they have knowledge of what the students currently know and understand. Once they know where the students are through some basic assessments on monitoring tools, they can then plan accordingly.

Throughout the unit of work there will be the opportunity to gather data, through either formal assessments or informal assessments, which can be summative or formative. The data collected will inform the teachers as to the students' progress. It may also inform the teachers as to the effectiveness of their teaching practice. All subject areas will have assessment tasks in primary school and high school, so that teachers can record students' outcomes which will reflect their progress and hopefully an upward trajectory in their growth and learning. These monitoring tools may be undertaken formally at the end of the unit, throughout the unit of work, or collected at periodic times throughout a term. Some schools still have the traditional exam block at the end of a term or semester during which time students will set a battery of tests and exams to provide information on their achievements, on their knowledge of the work undertaken in the preceding weeks and months. Without debating the merits of exam blocks or those of formative or summative assessment, it is safe to say that teachers have to collect data to reflect the child's ability and the child's progress.

Review and Response Meetings

Teachers' work must include the adjustments for students who require differentiation in their learning journey. Schools may employ the process of allowing teachers to meet with a colleague and learning support teachers and a member of the leadership team and undertake what may be called a review and response process. This is where the teacher would bring along work samples from a student who may not be progressing as expected. The teacher would share strategies they have already employed and their struggle to see any growth in that student's learning. The collective wisdom of the group would then offer suggestions as to how the teacher might address that student's learning. The collective wisdom would hopefully give new ideas to that teacher by which they may use strategies to see that student progress. This is an invaluable opportunity for peer-to-peer sharing of ideas with support of learning support experts, as well as the leadership.

Feedback to Teachers

Peer to peer feedback is a very important strategy by which teachers can learn from their colleagues. When a peer is seeking some peer feedback, it means that someone who is their equal is in a position to offer feedback that can be constructive and affirming. Ideally, the teacher can improve their practice.

When a member of leadership gives feedback, it is often of a constructive nature and teachers may find that initially somewhat threatening, particularly if they're not used to it. Hence the advantage of having peer to peer feedback means that a teacher may receive constructive feedback more positively. When teachers work collaboratively in planning, teaching, assessing and reporting, the opportunity for feedback creates a culture of trust and collaboration whereby teachers are encouraged and motivated to improve their practice. There will also be some teachers who may not feel confident giving feedback or feel unworthy of offering observations to their peers. These teachers maybe the untapped heroes of their teaching teams. Encouragement and an expectation of peer feedback may see them share their wisdom, albeit reluctantly at first.

If a peer has invited a colleague to give them feedback, they may wish to identify specific professional behaviours or pedagogy that they want critiqued. This gives the observing peer teacher direction to know what to look for and hence give the practitioner some specific feedback. This is really powerful. So peer-to-peer feedback is an important role of the class teacher. This also emphasises that all teachers are responsible for all learners in a school. Teachers need to think beyond their class and think beyond operating in a silo to their collective responsibilities for the teaching and the learning processes of all students. Learning doesn't only happen in classrooms, learning happens beyond the classroom. Teachers who have taught a student for a year and then hand that student over to their colleagues for the following year have a responsibility to share their knowledge, wisdom and expertise about a particular student. When teachers analyse data on student learning, teachers from previous years can reflect upon what was successful for them. Teachers who are currently teaching their class may reflect and discuss pedagogy that is successful or unsuccessful for the current cohort of students, as a collective and also as individual students.

Formative and Summative Assessment

There are two regular processes in the assessment of student learning: formative and summative assessment techniques. Dylan Wiliam (2017), a world-renowned expert in formative assessment, suggests that children can be assessed continually throughout a unit of work or throughout a school semester. Formative assessment would give the teacher feedback on how their teaching is impacting on a student's ability to learn a new concept. Summative assessment is often used at the conclusion of a unit of work, or the conclusion of a term or semester. It is important that teachers only assess what has been taught and that the data they gather from the assessments informs their teaching practice, as it will identify gaps in students' learning or their understanding. Both formative and summative assessments are very much part and parcel of education journey for both students and teachers.

Correcting and Marking

To prepare feedback for students, teachers have to spend time correcting and marking the students' work. The work should be marked against the Australian curriculum standards for each year level. Students may be graded against what is expected at each year level. The work corrected should be assessed as AT, ABOVE or BELOW the expected level. Using a five-point rating scale, teachers may have some students who are WELL BELOW or WELL ABOVE the expected standard for their year level. The younger students may not produce the volume of work that older students are expected to produce, so the time required to correct and mark work may vary, depending on the year level being taught. The majority of a teacher's correcting and marking would be done outside of the nine to three hours that teachers teach.

While school leaders may not have to correct and mark students' work, they may be involved in moderating work samples with the teachers. This ensures a degree of consistency of judgement within a cohort of teachers. This means that teachers making judgement on students' work should be making similar judgements. An ABOVE sample of work in one teacher's class should be marked at ABOVE by teachers in the same year level, if possible. Consistency of judgement is important so parents and teachers have confidence that regardless of which teacher a student has, their work is being assessed in a consistent and reliable manner.

It is most likely that school leaders will be reading the report cards that are prepared by the teachers to reflect the students' progress over a term or semester or a year. It takes many, many hours to read, correct and moderate results, and ensure the comments and marks are aligned. Then there is the feedback to the teachers, with the expectations that the teachers correct any errors and reflect on comments and marks. Each school leader may have their own preference as to how report card comments are written if the teachers write their own prose. Some education authorities have generated a bank of report comments from which the teachers can draw subject-specific comments. They are likely to write own their general comments for each individual student. Reports usually reflect effort, academic results, behaviour/conduct for all subjects that students are studying. In secondary schools, teachers of each subject will complete their assessment of students' work. In primary school, class teachers will plan, teach, assess, and report on most subjects, except for those subjects that are taught by specialist teachers, such as Music, Languages, Health and Physical Education and Art.

Reporting and Feedback to Parents

An important part of the teaching and learning processes is monitoring students' progress and reporting back to the parents. During the year, teachers are generally expected to have a minimum of two opportunities to provide formal feedback of children's progress to parents. It's common for schools to have an opportunity in Term 1, whereby the teacher may meet with the parents, understand the parents' knowledge of their own child and set some learning goals for the student. Ideally the student could be part of these meetings which are often referred to as student-led parent-teacher conferences. During the year there would be another opportunity by which the student-led conferences can have the student's progress discussed in more detail. Samples of the students' work will be used as the basis for the conversation, with the teacher sharing results. The student may discuss how they have progressed towards achieving their goals that were set earlier in the year. There may be occasions where schools feel more comfortable with just the parent teacher meeting taking place without the student being involved. It is the student's learning that is being discussed, hence there is great merit in having the student as part of student-led parent-teacher conferences.

Not all teachers are comfortable with this model of student-led parent/teacher conferences, and not all parents are comfortable with this model as they may want to discuss the student's progress in some detail and depth without the student understanding the adult language being used. The process of giving parents feedback about their child's learning is very important. Of course, there may be the need to have more regular meetings between parents and teachers regarding a particular child's progress. This can be done as frequently as the parents or the teachers deem necessary. Students with particular learning needs may also have what are called individual education plan meetings and reviews (they may be called educational adjustment programs for review). Any individual program through which a student may be supported should require more frequent meetings than just twice a year.

The preparation that is necessary to provide accurate feedback on a child's progress is significant. It is certainly a reasonable expectation that teachers would have samples of work as the basis for their judgements and share this with the parents. It is also preferable that there be no surprises at a parent-teacher interview. If a parent has been kept up to date on their child's progress throughout the year, then there should be no surprises at a parent-teacher interview. This should allow the teacher to feel very comfortable and confident in the message that they have to convey during the formal parent-teacher interview. These interviews are often held after hours, before school sometimes into the early evening. Some schools allow teachers to spend time on a weekend, offering the parents the chance to come and meet with them, if that is a more mutually convenient time. This may make having leadership support on site a challenge. Whatever the time provided for the parent teacher interviews, it is encouraged and expected that parents participate, so that they can support their child and their learning journey, and support the school in achieving their student's goals.

Enrichment Activities for the Gifted and Talented

Schools are often very good at providing support for the students who find academics challenging. Schools are becoming more proficient at also providing enriching activities for the high flyers of our academic student population. All students deserve to be challenged at school and to be enriched and excited by their learning journey. Students who find the learning of the standard curriculum too easy may often display poor behaviour. They may get bored at school, so it is important that teachers provide enriching activities to stretch children academically and in other ways. All students can be stretched academically. It's also important they can be stretched broadly, so that other opportunities may enhance their learning journey not just the pure academics. This may mean providing instrumental music programs, it may mean chess programs, it may mean artistic pursuits, or problem-solving activities. Programs such as Opti-MINDS and Tournament of Minds are examples of specific opportunities which schools may use for their brightest students. These are often facilitated and supervised by teachers and parents, after hours. While there is an element of competition as teams compete against each other, these programs are designed to provide students to problem solve, innovate, work as a team, think creatively as they work through problems.

Whatever opportunities are provided for students, they must be engaging, life-giving and exciting to stimulate a child to want to learn and also to stretch them academically. Schools may employ teachers for gifted and talented programs or enrichment programs. Whatever they are called, schools should provide opportunities for these students, to have their learning stretched and supported so they can be challenged. All students have the right to move forward in their academic progress so even if students are already at or above their expected year level standards, they should be stretched beyond where they currently start a school year. That's a great challenge for teachers and for enrichment teachers and teachers of the gifted and talented students, and leadership teams. **Remember, it is our mandated responsibility to ensure that all children can learn and can progress in the learning journey**.

Learning Support Including Referrals and Recording Adjustments

Part and parcel of any good teacher's job is to differentiate the curriculum so that all students have access to learning. To differentiate the curriculum means making and recording adjustments to ensure that students can access the curriculum. Frequently these are students who may have needs that warrant individual education plans or educational adjustment plans, whereby the teachers will make changes to ensure that the students can still learn at their level and strive to improve beyond where they are currently. This is a very time-consuming task yet is necessary so that all students can learn at their individual level. Now is it realistic to expect a teacher to have 25 or 30 individual learning plans for their class? No. Is it realistic to expect that a teacher will differentiate the learning for groups of students who are of similar ability? Absolutely. And is it necessary? Absolutely.

The Australian government has a process called Nationally Consistent Collection of Data (NCCD), whereby they like to understand the needs of the students in our schools and the adjustments that are necessary according to frequency and intensity. There are four categories in NCCD: they are **quality teacher differentiated programs (QDTP)** which is just what any good practitioner will employ on a daily basis. There are students whose needs would meet the requirements for **supplementary** support in so far adjustments would be made for some subjects for on some occasions. There are students who would require some **substantial** adjustments for much of the day for much of the week. There are students who require adjustments that are quite **extensive** and these would be students who may have almost one-on-one support at school. These categories are based on the frequency, intensity and type of adjustments that teachers make. The recording of such adjustments takes significant time. It is up to the classroom teacher to make the adjustments and record them on their unit plans while being supported by the learning support teachers. The leadership team, often the principal, signs off on what they believe are the accepted levels of student adjustments, before the database of students on NCCD goes to a moderation panel for confirming of the level of adjustments. Part of the monitoring and recording of the adjustments is also the engagement with external agencies and conversations with the parents of students who have such adjustments made.

This consultation and collaborative process is very important and it highlights the fact that education is a journey of collaboration between the parents and the teachers. It is also emphasising that collaboration between external expert providers is important so that the school can do its best to meet the students' needs, with the support of external agencies. Students who had such adjustments made often require regular meetings between parents and teachers so that goals can be set, so that strategies may be developed, so that goals can be discussed and that progress can be monitored. Teachers who have multiple students who require adjustments may be asked to have regular meetings with many families throughout a school term, or school semester or a school year. This can be quite an exhausting process, both emotionally and physically for a teacher who is invested in students, especially those who may have learning needs.

Liaising with External Agencies

There are numerous external professionals that teachers and school leaders have to work with to provide a most fulsome support for students. Such experts in their field may include allied health workers such as speech therapists, occupational therapists, visiting teachers for hearing impairment and physical impairment. Experts in the fields of Indigenous students, refugees and migrants are also key external support networks. These specialists may work in schools to provide intervention for students with specific needs, that impact on their ability to access the curriculum. These needs may have often been identified through the teaching and learning process. It is to everyone's advantage when teachers, school leaders and allied health workers collaborate on common strategies to address the agreed goals for the student. The cooperation and collaboration means that a holistic approach to attending to students' needs is possible. There are occasions where these allied health workers may work on site at school. This allows for close communication between teachers and allied health workers. On other occasions students may attend therapy off site. Either way school staff and these experts need to work together. Now while the core business of schools is teaching and learning, the optimal time for therapy is the morning, which is also the optimal learning time at school. To maximise the learning time and the expert intervention, therapy at school and feedback between teachers and therapists may occur on the school site. (A word of caution: ideas for strategies at school suggested by therapists need to be actioned by the teacher, in the context of their class practices. And hence the context for implementation of classroom strategies must be manageable within the classroom. Some suggestions are workable, while others may be most effective in other settings).

Some students come from fragile home lives that may require the intervention of other experts, beyond their family and beyond the school staff. Some students who are at risk of harm require intervention and support from various government departments, such as the Department of Family Services. It is the responsibility of these departments to ensure the safety and wellbeing of the students if their families are not willing or able. School staff need to understand what is impacting a student's ability to concentrate at school and if that means understanding the student's personal life in some details, without breaking privacy laws, then that's a good idea.

There maybe students who are in the care of the state, i.e. in the sanctioned care of foster carers. These carers have case workers and the children often have support workers. There may be numerous stakeholders involved in the care of such children. At school the teachers will continue in their role of providing high-quality teaching and learning, while the school leaders may provide them with information on a need-to-know basis. These are complex situations which require some astute management from the school leaders. Teachers generally wish to teach and often prefer the complex situations to be handled by those with higher pay scales.

Permission Forms and Risk Assessments

Some teachers are very conscientious in providing opportunities for students beyond the classroom and beyond the hours of work. There are many opportunities for children to participate in activities outside of school hours and some teachers are very generous in their time and energy to provide such opportunities. Some of these might be community activities such as the local community Anzac Day March, whereby staff may agree to meet families in a particular designated point for a community march, supervise the students during the march, assist the students in laying a wreath at any ceremony, and then assist in finding their parents so they can be handed back to their families at the end of the march.

Some staff are quite happy to train students outside of school time for various sporting activities and then even lead them in after school activities or after school competitions. Some school staff do get paid for these extracurricular opportunities, while staff working in other educational jurisdictions will not be paid for these opportunities. Associated with the actual activity is the paperwork to be completed. Risk assessments and permission forms are part and parcel of the life of a teacher. Approving such documents often falls to a member of the leadership team to ensure that all the factors have been considered when planning such events and that all risks are minimised and that maximum opportunity is provided in a safe environment. Communication must be clear and concise to the family so that students can have maximum participation.

There is significant paperwork required of teachers when planning excursions and incursions. Schools may have 'excursion/incursion request' forms that teachers are expected to complete. These are to include the rationale for the activity and the curriculum links. Someone from the leadership team would have the delegated authority to approve or question the activity. There are numerous criteria that leadership would use to make a determination about the suitability of each activity. Such criteria will include:

- Relevance to the curriculum
- Value for money
- Time away from school vs the time spent on the activity
- Travel time and age of students
- Originality of activity (has it been done before?)

Once the activity has the support of leadership, the teacher would then be expected to do a risk assessment. This assessment should include all elements of the activity, including travel arrangements, supervision, students' behaviour, staff participation, medication management, volunteers, toileting arrangements, photography arrangements. Risk assessments will record who is responsible for the various elements of the activity. Risk assessments take time and some teachers would rather not do an excursion/incursion to avoid the paperwork, and the minimise the possibility of anything going wrong by avoiding the activity. This is the sad reality for some teachers. Once all the paperwork has been completed, a member of the leadership team will have the delegated authority check it. Occasionally the review of the paperwork may reveal some omissions that the teachers need to include. Once everything is signed and sealed the detailed planning may begin, including distribution of permission forms (hopefully electronic), details of activity's venue, rationale, arrangement of transport, coordinating volunteers (including checking that the volunteers have done their Code of Conduct training). The value of such activities should add to the teaching and learning and teachers should be encouraged to explore ways to bring the curriculum alive through hands on experiences where possible and appropriate.

Parent Engagement

Another important role that teachers have to play is to build healthy, positive relationships with the parents of their students. Communication with parents needs to be two-way. It needs to be informative, positive and life-giving for both the teacher and the parents. Invariably much of the communication that takes place between parents and teachers has to happen outside of school hours by virtue of teachers doing their job, teaching students between 8:30 a.m. and 3 p.m. approximately. It is a reasonable expectation that teachers will keep parents informed on the student's learning journey. It is also reasonable to expect that parents will keep teachers informed about anything that may impact student's ability to learn and access the curriculum. Building a positive relationship between parents and teachers is important because research will tell us that parents who are engaged with their child's learning journey will have better outcomes for the child themselves (Waterford Education, 2023). So communication between parents and teachers is highly important to a positive impact on learning for students.

Relationships between parents and teachers don't always run smoothly as with any relationship. Yet it is important that a culture of trust and collaboration is created between parents and teachers. As such it is important that parents and teachers have a common goal because they're working for the child, which is the person they have in common and have a vested interest in from a parental point-of-view and from a teacher's point of view.

Promoting parent engagement and parent involvement in school life is also a key part of providing high-quality teaching and learning for all students. Now this does not mean that parents have to be at school every day doing reading groups or working in the canteen or going on excursions. It should mean that parents are kept abreast of what is happening in their child's class through regular communication, through participating in the child's homework, reading the newsletters or social media posts, or providing feedback to the teachers on their child's progress. There are many ways the parents can get involved in their child's school life without having to be on site at school every other day. We certainly need parents to be involved at school. However, given that many parents are working it is often necessary for parents to engage with their child's learning after hours. The key message for teachers is that they must create a positive environment in which parents are welcome to be a part of the educational journey of their child. This is an investment in the child's education and creating the positive relationship is an investment in building a culture of trust and collaboration.

Physical Classroom

Another example of how teachers can have a positive influence in the classroom is how furniture can enhance or restrict current pedagogical practices. Conversely pedagogy can influence the furniture that schools will purchase. Teachers and school leaders need to work collaboratively to identify what is the best way to deliver the curriculum to meet the needs of the students. School leaders have the potential to influence the pedagogy that's practised and hence the furniture that may be bought to support the pedagogical practice. Now it's not uncommon for some schools to buy furniture and hope the pedagogy changes. It is more preferable to change the pedagogy and then buy the furniture which will accommodate the pedagogy. That's another example of how teachers and school leaders need to work collaboratively to drive the core business of teaching and learning. It's also an example of how school leaders are influential in the teaching-learning process. Very basic and very important.

Resources

When teachers are planning, the school leader would make the expectation that there will be collaboration among colleagues. School leaders may determine that the resources used must be in line with current pedagogical practices. There may be debate around the use of textbooks in schools, or any alternative resource. The school leaders may in fact determine the level of photocopying and the use of paper that is used in classrooms. Leaders and teachers may also discuss those types of resources the staff may use. They may also determine how technology is used in modern classrooms. Should students be on one-to-one devices from the early years in primary school or should one-to-one devices be held over until the upper years of primary school? That's another example of how a school leader can influence the direction of the pedagogy in their particular school. Teachers and school leaders must work together to drive the pedagogical direction of the school to ensure that all students can access the curriculum.

In a recent survey of some colleagues and my staff, the data indicated that opinions are very much divided on the place of text books in a modern classroom. Some teachers are adamant that using a textbook will save copying. Possibly true. Textbooks can also be sent home to be used to reinforce a previously taught concept. Possibly true. The downside is that textbooks are not individualised for the specific needs of students. While some students may benefit from using textbooks, other students would find them unnecessary and a waste of time and money. If parents are asked to invest in textbooks, there is likely the expectation that the books will be used and not left idle for the majority of the year. This debate will rage for years to come and there is no easy answer, especially when individual teachers cannot agree on best practice ... yet.

Summary Statement

The core business of educators is to provide high-quality teaching and learning for all students. It is a collaborative endeavour between school leaders, teachers, support staff and families. Teaching is a complex process that often requires teachers to work after hours.

School leaders are a vital cog in ensuring that teachers meet their obligations in planning, teaching, assessing and reporting. It is a challenge and one which most educators embrace with a passion. It is getting harder as expectations rise.

The numerous elements in providing high-quality teaching and learning are competing with the various demands of society and often educators themselves. Teaching and learning should be life-giving for the teachers and the students. It must be done in collaboration with the parents. It must also be based on effective pedagogies while covering the Australian curriculum.

JUGGLING STRATEGIES

- Enable collaborative opportunities for peer-to-peer observations.

- Prioritise learning walks and talks to know the students and their progress, and to know the teacher's impact on the students' learning progress.

- Practise goal setting with the teachers to guide them to identify ways to improve their practice to have greater impact on the students' progress.

- Provide regular and timely feedback to the teachers so they can be supported in improving their practice to have greater impact on the students' progress.

- Invest in personnel that impact on teaching, such as literacy coaches, teacher mentors, principal mentors.

"

Know the research
Focus on the learning
Know thy impact

John Hattie

2

Expectations and Duties of Educators

In late 2021 I was interviewed for the position of principal at a primary school in Brisbane. This school had over 100 years of history, located in a high socio-economic part of the city and consistently achieved excellent NAPLAN results. During the interview the panel discussed the upcoming building project and explored my experience in managing similar projects. Towards the end of the interview the employing authority's Director on the panel asked me to guess what would he advise me about building projects. I correctly replied, 'not to let the building project distract me from my core business of teaching and learning'. I was successful in being appointed to that school and now over 12 months into my contract, I can reveal that while I knew that was the politically correct response, the reality may be somewhat different. I knew that if principals were not working closely with architects and builders, then the final product may not be what the school needs. This is just one example of one of the many tasks that school principals may engage with, that take time and 'distract' principals from their core business.

This chapter will explore the many and varied activities that may occupy a principal's time beyond the core business of teaching and learning.

The reality is that school leaders are often distracted or have their time occupied by numerous other important aspects of school life. Let's unpack some of those important elements that occupy school leaders' time and often teachers' time.

Pastoral Care

Quite often school leaders are the first port of call when families are in crisis. This can be relationship breakdowns, illness or bereavements of family members that require the support of caring leaders. Often the teachers and the school leadership team are some of the support mechanisms that families call on in times of crisis. When a family appears unannounced at a principal's door and asks for their time and bursts into tears while sharing the story of a bereavement or the relationship breakdown or the illness of a child, the principal in their pastoral nature may feel that they can support that family, if not at least personally, then through providing contacts through other mechanisms such as school guidance counsellors or even external agencies. It is common that principals and deputy principals and guidance counsellors are the trusted people in families' lives who are called upon to provide support in times of need. When such events happen families often turn to the people who care about their children the most, and that is often the staff at the child's school. The support that can be provided by schools may purely be of a pastoral nature. Guidance counsellors may provide more professional support and be able to direct the family to the external agencies that can provide more professional and targeted support. I do recognise and applaud the work of all guidance counsellors and pastoral workers because the work they carry out in responding to a variety of needs of students, families and staff is quite extraordinary.

While the possible support of families may not necessarily fall under the role description of the school staff, it is certainly in the nature of many teachers and school leaders to provide pastoral care as needed by families. A bereavement of a family member attached to a school can take many hours of support for a family, both in the lead up to the funeral as well as supporting a family post funeral. Providing meals through the school care and concern networks is quite a common practice. It takes time to ensure that school fees are managed if families run into financial difficulty or that support is provided when family relationships break down. Impartial support is crucial, without passing judgement on either parent, who may or may not be at fault. These are examples of how school leaders' time can be taken up with pastoral care.

Pastoral issues may also extend to staff. Bereavements, illnesses, relationship breakdowns are all part and parcel of people's lives. If a staff member is struggling with any of these issues, deputies and principals are often called upon to provide support. This support could in fact be facilitating the staff member to take leave so they can address their personal issues. The staff member may feel that work is the best place for them to be to occupy their time. Is this the right decision? That's for the individual staff and leadership to manage and to digest. There is no manual on how best to support people through such crises yet when pastoral support is required of staff members then the leadership team often step up and support their staff. In extreme cases there may be the death of a staff member or the death of a spouse of a staff member. Staff members may be having psychological crisis and not being able to fulfil their job. Relationship breakdowns on staff will also take some time to work through for the relevant people. It would be saddening to know that pastoral care for staff is ever questioned when it takes up the time of the leaders of a school.

Parents and Citizens Meetings and Board Meetings

It is common for schools to have one, if not two, parent leadership groups, and often more in high schools. For example, there may be parents and friends (P&F) or parents and citizens (P&C) associations in schools whereby the parents may offer their time and energy to fundraise for the school. Such associations often have monthly meetings or sub-committee meetings per term, at which time and place the principal or deputy would attend and provide reports and guidance on operational matters as required by the association. Such associations are often charged with raising funds directed towards school projects. What school projects they would fund should be at the discretion of the leadership team and the staff, as they have the overall picture of the school and know where funds need to be directed. High-functioning P&F or P&C associations add great value to schools and as such should be energising for the school leadership team. Often these meetings are after hours and held in the evening so that working parents can be involved. Principals or deputies often prepare reports for such meetings, taking time in giving the school overview of projects coming up or priorities that the P&F may need to address at their monthly meetings. There are very clear guidelines as to the jurisdiction under which P&F associations should operate and as to what they are mandated to address. Clarifying such issues is time consuming, particularly when new P&F associations are led by inexperienced executive members. However, I would like to repeat that high functioning P&F associations add great value to schools and are often a tremendous support for the school leadership team.

Another group that primary schools may have are school boards. Such boards are often not governance boards, they may be advisory boards to the school principal. These groups would have meetings that are held at least once or twice each term, often monthly. At the selected time and place, the principal would present a report about what is happening in the school and what school's vision is. There should be clear guidelines of what projects the school board should be undertaking, which are often long-term, visionary, policy planning type decisions. Members of boards should not be coming with their own personal agendas and they should be representative of the broader school community. If schools have a board of governance they have different purpose and that may be as a hiring and firing type board that oversee the leadership of the school. There is preparation required by the school principal to ensure that they keep the board informed of all matters relevant to their roles. This takes time.

The other parent groups that often work in high schools are parent support groups. For example, there may be the rowing parent support group or the music support group or the cricket support group or the creative arts support group. These groups provide leadership for the school and the parents, to ensure that school activities can run smoothly as they are often extracurricular activities. Ideally these groups take some of the time and energy required from teachers, and often the school leadership team, to ensure that these activities can still be provided for the students. It is quite common that staff be involved with such groups so that these parent groups cannot function without the support and guidance of the school. This requires time outside of school where parents meet, with support from staff, to ensure that their specific projects can be planned and actioned to continue providing high-quality opportunities for the students.

Workplace Health and Safety Matters

As the person ultimately responsible for the health and safety of all visitors to their school, principals should oversee all workplace health and safety matters. It's quite common practice for schools now to have a Workplace Health and Safety Committee (WHS Committee) comprising staff, parents and members from the leadership team. From my experience, these committees meet frequently per term to address any workplace health and safety issues and to ensure that all mandatory requirements are fulfilled, verifying that the safety and wellbeing of all visitors, students, staff and families are managed at the school site. This committee often has to review policies and practices in the school, particularly as policies and practices may change from the governing authority or governments. For example, when governing authorities determine that risk assessments need to include various components, then the Workplace Health and Safety Committee should ensure that all staff are made aware of such changes. When accidents and injuries occur on site, it is important that the WHS Committee monitor and track the management of such injuries and accidents, to minimise their impact at schools. This may require the principal and the grounds staff doing regular inspections of the school to check playgrounds, to check all aspects of WHS. However, with legislation changing frequently, it is nearly impossible for principals to be kept abreast of the latest requirements. Hence, they often require the support from the governing authorities to have WHS advisors to ensure that knowledge and skills can be kept up-to-date. In some education sectors, there is workplace health and safety training that all staff have to do, at least on an annual basis. Certainly, as changes are made to mandatory requirements, then staff must be kept informed of such change that impacts their work.

You'll notice a theme appearing: like the other bodies mentioned, the WHS Committee usually meets outside of school hours. Let me ask the question now as we're exploring all these additional responsibilities as to **how much time should school leaders and teachers be investing in before-and-after-school activities that are not related to teaching-learning?** Now, it could be argued that WHS is essential to teaching and learning. We need a safe environment to fulfil our obligations. Ultimately, it is the principal's responsibility because if things do go wrong then the principal will be asked to explain their policies, practices, protocols, procedures and processes. If they cannot prove that all measures were undertaken to minimise and to mitigate the risk associated with working at school, then their conduct may be questioned.

Staffing

As a school year approaches it is imperative that the schools have a full complement of staff. While that sounds relatively straightforward, and you would assume that once a school year kicks off, staffing issues would be minimal. In reality managing people, is an ongoing matter for school leaders, week in week out. Certainly, in the second half of the year as principals are preparing for the following school year, ensuring that all staffing is in place does take time. It's a big challenge for school leaders to allocate sufficient budget to hire numerous competent staff. Once the leadership team, the school board and staff come to an accepted position on what roles they will have in the school and how many staff they will have on site for the following year, then the school leadership go about ensuring those positions are filled. Finding staff replacement for various roles can be an arduous task. For example, the process would involve advertising the position, providing an accurate role description, reviewing and short-listing applications, arranging the interviews, taking time to brief the interview panel and interviewing applicants.

If a principal has more than one position to fill, it can take literally weeks to months to ensure that staff are in place. Who is involved in the staffing process is based on the principal's discretion. In some big schools, deputy principal can run this process and inform the principal. In smaller schools, the principal might be involved in every interview. Support staff can also arrange interviews and call interview candidates. These processes are certainly left to the discretion of the school principal, as to how they wish to manage the whole staffing process.

On a day-to-day, week-to-week basis, the management team should see that staff are fulfilling their duties and role statements, keeping them accountable. This does require supervision, including feedback to the staff, after the required monitoring. Again, this takes time and when school leaders have to determine how best to spend their time, this should be a high priority. Investing time in the teachers and support staff who are going to have most impact on the teaching-learning process is vital. In all reality most teachers do a fantastic job, as do most support staff and hence the need to monitor and supervise those teachers may not be as great as teachers who are struggling to fulfil their duties. All staff deserve feedback on their work. It could be affirmations to give them due recognition for the great job they're doing. It could be critical feedback which gives them areas for further improvement. Again, this takes time and it's a key role for school leaders.

School leaders need to manage staff who are underperforming and struggling to meet the job demands, which is one of the most emotionally draining and challenging responsibilities. Consider the time required to provide feedback, negotiate realistic goals to create improvements, following up with them and possibly engaging with union representatives. In the worst case scenario, school leaders might have to usher them out, which can be a taxing and uncomfortable situation. It is also one of the reasons why underperforming staff often continue in schools because the process to manage out underperforming staff is exhausting. If a staff member is doing the bare minimum that is required according to the union or according to their role description, there is very little schools can do encourage them to exceed expectations. If the teacher does not have the desire to improve, then the time and energy invested by school leaders can often be wasted. This of course is extended to managing teaching staff and support staff, along with office staff, grounds staff, any specialist onsite. Anybody who is in the paid employment of a particular school needs to be managed and supervised so that they add to the value of the school.

High performing schools will have high performing staff who have their own personal and professional goals and will continue to strive for professional improvements. Schools that have staff that have retired mentally yet keep turning up for work physically, create a huge challenge for school leaders to manage. It is a responsibility of school leaders to ensure that all students have access to high-quality teaching and learning.

Budgets and Financial Management

Managing a school's budget requires prudent financial leadership on behalf of the principal with the support of finance officers. Schools are possibly running budgets of many hundreds of thousands of dollars, or tens of millions of dollars. The responsibility remains the same in so far as there should be prudent allocation and spending of school funds, providing an excellent standard of education for every student. If governing authorities require budgets to be approved early in the second half of the year or at the start of a financial year for the following calendar year, this means that schools need to have their budgets in place months in advance of the following school year. This requires great planning and preparation and an understanding of the vision for the school.

We've already mentioned the impact staffing that can have on budgets. So too can capital spending, resourcing, maintenance, administrative costs, utilities - the same that are required in household budgets. All of these things need to be projected forward, often based on enrolment numbers, so that their sound financial position can be determined, to allow school leaders and finance officers to do some prudent planning. Such preparation requires meticulous attention to detail, a feasible vision, understanding of the consequences in the near future, a degree of mathematical ability and accurate computer skills often using programs such as Excel with formulae that can be replicated to deal with changing numbers in enrolments, staffing and grants. It is often cause for consternation as to how budgets are determined, who has the final say in budgets, and where the priorities are positioned. Often this comes down to the leadership team, with input from teachers, and the school board. Ultimately it is the educators who need to prioritise where funds should be directed. These directions may include resourcing various specialists within the school, such as music teachers, PE teachers, language teachers, teacher librarians, support teachers, guidance counsellors, religion teachers and curriculum leaders. All of these people may wish to have their own individual budgets. Classroom teachers may also wish to have budgets so that they can manage for their own class priorities, particularly when spending on discretionary items such as consumables and planning for curriculum school-based excursions. How all these figures are determined and worked out is often a great mystery to families and staff. Hence it is encouraged that the process by which principals undertake such activities should be transparent so that there are no surprises and no mismanagement of school funds. Not all principals would like to manipulate excel spreadsheets and hence they may require the support of finance officers who may also require the support of finance officers from the governing authorities.

When principals and deputies sit down with an Excel spreadsheet with multiple tabs and their table of numbers, it can be quite daunting to make sense of the impact that every child and every staff member may have on the allocation of funds. Hence school leaders are encouraged to be very transparent in the processes, so people can understand the complexities in managing school budgets. High schools have the benefit of having business managers, often qualified accountants, who are trained in this process, even though the final responsibility may rest with the principal. Primary school principals are often left to their own devices when they are managing multimillion-dollar budgets. This comes with great responsibility so that there is prudent management of funds.

Marketing

One of the challenges for all school leaders is to attract enrolments to their school. The way any business attracts patronage is by marketing and sound promotion. Similarly within education, school leaders or deputies or board members need to find ways in which they can market and promote what their school has to offer to ensure the long-term viability of their schools. From my experience this is becoming more and more challenging when parents are faced with a plethora of schools to choose from. Now some principals and deputies have a great passion for marketing and hence may have some ideas about ways in which they can attract enrolments. Other principals have very few ideas about how they can attract enrolments and hence often require the support of external people. Marketing can include having activities such as open days, parent evenings, advertisements on social and print media. Trying to identify schools' individual features should be relatively straightforward, yet most schools offer similar curricula. The philosophy should be similar from school to school, especially those under the same governing bodies. One of the great dilemmas for school leaders is to identify their point-of-difference. What makes their school different and better than their neighbouring schools? How can school leaders send that message out to the broader community to acquire people's interest and see what they have to offer?

It's common for schools to be able to entice people once their interests are piqued. The challenge is convincing families to enrol their children into the school. There are certainly marketing experts who can be contracted to promote schools. Yet the impact of marketing strategies may not be seen for a year or two. This becomes quite a challenging undertaking when financial investments are made while waiting a long time to see resulting outcomes. Certainly, the use of social media these days is a very common practice in which schools can promote their success stories. Open days still exist in many schools, whereby parents can visit schools either during the weekday when school is functioning or on weekends when students may come back and host such an event, with the leadership of staff. These activities still require leadership from the school leadership team and often teachers and often support staff. If the school is just functioning and the open days are filled, teachers will often go out of their way to represent an outstanding image of the school, showcasing students doing extraordinary things. However, these impact can only be fully seen months or years after implementing the marketing strategy. This is a real challenge for schools to get their heads around, because they will make an investment for multiple years and not see any change for many years.

Promotion of your school often involves using images of current students. Professional photo shoots take time and money, identifying students who have media permission (i.e. parental permission for their children's images to be used and seen in the public domain), identifying settings for the promotional pictures, supervising the photo shoot, choosing the best images, selecting the appropriate platform on which to promote the school. Note that not all schools will need or use marketing campaigns as their reputation is enough to attract enrolments.

While schools under the same governing authority, such as an education body, may not believe they are in competition with each other, the reality is every school competing directly for enrolments. While the Australian curriculum is set by the Australian government and while schools can have their own unique curriculum offerings above and beyond the Australian curriculum, in all reality schools are in competition with each other to attract enrolments, which attract funding. I'm not sure of how many principals or deputies have marketing degrees and yet it is often left to the school to invest their time and energy in promoting their own offerings.

Enrolments

Schools can only exist if they have students, whom they are going to educate. Every enrolment has an impact on staffing levels. Hence, enrolments are critical to the success of schools (financial viability, and possibility of providing a variety of resources and programs). The enrolment process often follows on from the marketing strategy. If we can get people through the front doors of their school, then we have the opportunity to walk them through the enrolment process. Those schools that have waiting lists and operate often with outstanding long histories and no need to chase enrolments yet still have huge marketing budgets, may not need to invest in the enrolment process as much as schools that struggle to attract families to their front door. Once we have families at our schools, then the enrolment process can be undertaken.

On occasion families will just engage with the school website, complete enrolment forms, submit and wait for the formal face-to-face process to commence. The management of the paperwork should be left to the enrolment officers. The process for meeting families and meeting prospective students is often left to the leadership team. Now the actual process will vary from school to school. Ideally there should be the opportunity for every prospective family to meet with a member of the staff to discuss the student and their needs and to promote the school. Some principals may choose not to work this process for siblings of existing students, given that most schools have the policy that siblings are an automatic entry once there is a brother or sister already in attendance. My philosophy is that **every child** has their own unique needs and deserves to have the enrolment process in its entirety, to be supported with full knowledge of their needs. Now enrolment interviews can range anywhere from 10 to 45 minutes, depending on the student's needs. There would be some standard questions that most principals would ask the parents and there'd be some questions that principals would ask the students. These could even be to our youngest primary school students, who may be only three and a half to four years of age. Now if you work in a larger school seeing 100 incoming students every intake year, for example in the preparatory year, consider the time and effort to conduct those interviews. If you multiply 150 interviews by on average 20 minutes, you can estimate the number of hours invested in enrolling families.

Following the initial interview, any student who has been identified with exceptional learning needs would need follow-up conversations so that their supported enrolment can be enacted faithfully. Straightforward interviews that don't require any follow-up, may take a total of an hour of investment from the starting point of processing paperwork, holding enrolment interviews, sending out letters of offer, collecting the paperwork back.

Now while the school principal doesn't have to do all that work, they are certainly encouraged to be involved in the enrolment interviews. Once the interviews have been done, then it may be required to prioritise applications so that the enrolments officer can send out letters of offer to the top priority families, who meet the first multiple criteria. There may be the need to respond to disappointed families who missed out on the offers. Principals are engaged in that process when the families may require more explanation as to why they weren't offered a position and hence the enrolment officer defers any response onto the principal. Schools that are chasing enrolments would wish to have this problem, whereas schools that have a waiting list invariably deal with this problem on an annual basis. Enrolments are crucial and considerably time-consuming, since we need to ensure that every process is met fairly with transparent and thorough communication, so that families are welcomed into our schools.

The success of schools is built around the relationships between staff and families. This relationship starts at the point of enrolment. Prospective families will get a 'feel' of the school from their initial contact. Everyone who is involved in the enrolment process must be aware of the impact their presence has on the school's future families.

Assemblies

School assemblies occur frequently, either on a weekly, fortnightly or monthly basis. These can be based on year levels or entire school assemblies. Regardless of the frequency and the model of assembly, there is a lot of planning and factors to be taken into account. Often deputies or assistant principals will run the assemblies with the principal being present. Special assemblies for special occasions, such as Anzac Day or National Child Protection Week or NAIDOC Week or Christmas or Easter, require more investment of time and preparation. While assemblies certainly build school spirit and school-community relationships, the value to the teaching-learning process is arguably minimal. The time children spend sitting at assemblies and not doing anything beneficial to the teaching-learning process may also be questioned. Yet the value in celebrating successes and sharing stories and honouring people through processes such as assemblies, can be seen as important. It may be one of those discretionary activities that schools need to question when analysing the investment of time in school activities.

The exciting and unpredictable nature of an assembly, for example a Christmas decorating competition for the local shopping centre, can generate great interest of the students. Similarly, meeting with representatives from charitable organisations and presenting them with a gift for their underprivileged clients, may also be of great community service and build important links to the community, while having minimal links to the teaching and learning process. We cannot underestimate the value of connections to the community. We just need to juggle the best use of time and the best ways to build school/community spirit and connections. There are numerous ways in which schools can build connections with the broader community such as incursions, excursions, volunteering, attendance at events, promoting activities. Somehow principals have to determine which community groups they support and promote. All community groups have their profile and belief in their work. Schools need to act with judicial caution.

Capital and Building Works

As schools continue to improve their facilities, they will have to prioritise investing in capital projects. There will also be the investment in school improvements through annual maintenance projects such as cleaning and painting. Prioritising such endeavours takes time. Major building works such as the establishment of whole new schools or new buildings, still require a massive investment of time by the principal. Again, I'm unaware of how many principals would have done project management courses and yet there are occasions where principals meet with builders and architects to discuss the best way that project can be initiated, enacted and then concluded. How many principals would feel confident reading a building plan or negotiating with architects as to what is appropriate in a modern classroom, as opposed to what is a pretty design out of an architect's imagination or even out of an architect's experience? How does a principal facilitate and mediate and negotiate between architects and builders, one who is the theoretical designer, while the other remains the practical builder?

With the principal being the client, it is imperative to ensure that the students who will be occupying the building, have their needs met by the teachers who will be occupying the space with the students. Some teachers have no interest at all in capital projects and in what their new classroom may look like, while others might micromanage classrooms settings and yet that is not their responsibility. At some point the principals and their deputies have to work closely with building supervisors and architects and builders to ensure they get the best possible outcome, on budget and within a realistic timeframe. While it is preferable that principals don't micromanage the process, it is critical that principals do have a say on all major decisions. The design of classroom space is an important decision. The amount of storage and display space is a critical decision. The use of technology is a critical decision. The colour scheme, well that can be left up to people who worry about whether the walls are the right shade of blue or beige. Certainly, the layout and the functionality of the space are key decisions that school leaders must be involved with to ensure great outcomes.

Managing the financial aspect of such projects is an added complexity to the budgeting and financial management of the school. Schools that don't have capital projects are relatively straightforward in their financial management processes. Schools that have capital projects and require funding through grants or self-funded projects take significant time. It all takes time and energy. Principals must work closely with their finance officers to manage the building project. The financials include the payment of local authority approvals, professional fees for architects, engineers and building contractors. Any variations that may be paid independently to sub-contractors need to be paid. Schools may be paying all these expenses through their accounts or they may send them on to the education authority for payment on their behalf. Sounds simple and usually is, if everyone knows the process.

Student Protection Matters

One of the more complex and important responsibilities that school leaders have is the management of any student protection matter. There are mandatory requirements for schools to report causes of student harm and there are also the requirements that all schools ensure the safety and wellbeing of all their students. If a student does disclose a matter of safety and their welfare, then the person receiving that message has an obligation to listen and keep that student safe. There may be the need for an internal investigation and recording of details and processes. Schools frequently have student protection contacts who are nominated staff members and take the leadership role in managing student protection matters. Invariably principals should be one of the student protection contacts. It is quite common that guidance councillors are often a school's student protection contacts, and possibly deputies and or other full-time staff. Now I say full-time staff because it is important that students and parents and staff know that there will be at least one student protection contact onsite everyday (There may be exceptions when every student protection contact is away, so long as they are contactable). When a student makes a disclosure to a caring adult in a school, then there are processes and protocols that the listener must follow. It may mean going straight to the principal or other student protection contacts, sharing the story and handing over to them, at which time they will follow the expected processes.

Even principals and student protection contacts will then go to a higher authority to get further advice about how best to manage the disclosure. Schools often have a database in place where they can log a record of concern (ROC) to accurately note what has been reported by the student. There may be occasions where police are involved or the Department of Children, Youth Justice and Multicultural Affairs (or equivalent, depending on the geographical state's terminology; e.g. Department of Communities and Justice in New South Wales). The person receiving the disclosure needs to have confidence in the student protection contacts, that the due process will be followed to ensure the safety of the child. Once again there are mandatory reporting requirements and these may vary from state to state. The time it takes to deal with student protection matters is enormous. I usually say to my staff that if my office door is closed and I have to disappear for a day or two as result of the student protection matter, then please understand that it takes time to collect the information, get advice from the education authority experts, write up the ROC, ensure due process has been adhered to, follow up with the relevant department as required, to ensure the safety of a child. It is a child's safety that must be our first priority.

While reporting a disclosure may seem straightforward, the follow-up implications can be long-lasting. It's not uncommon for follow-up actions to happen months and in some cases years after the initial disclosure has been made. It's not uncommon for schools to get subpoenas requesting historical information based on allegations that were made years after the alleged event. Now while it is not the responsibility of the principal to sort through archive files, it is the responsibility of the principal to approve whatever information is being sent through to the governing authority or the courts. Such investigations and searching through school archives takes time.

All student protection matters must be taken seriously and must follow due process. While some teachers may feel concerned about reporting 'good' families for alleged harm, they may feel more concerned if they don't report 'good' families and something bad happens to a child. That's an important message that all staff need to understand – when a child says something we need to listen and it's better that an investigation happens and innocence is proven, as opposed to not reporting and harm be done to a child. No one wants harm done to a child and hence we have to ensure the safety of all students by following student protection processes. It all takes time and a child's welfare is the most important thing.

Summary Statement

How am I supposed to fit in everything that is asked of me as a teacher and school leader, within the working hours plus a reasonable amount of after-hours work? Planning, paperwork, finding resources, meeting with colleagues and parents, differentiating the curriculum, being compliant especially with WHS, recording student behaviours, student protection, planning assemblies, going on camps and excursions. Teachers may not have enough time to do everything, especially if they have a life outside of their work. If they are operating within a culture of trust and collaboration, then asking questions about how and why schools do certain activities should be a positive and reflective process. This then allows schools to prioritise their core business of teaching and learning. Some activities are important for community building and community engagement. Remember that when choosing what activities to keep and what to discard.

School leaders are often occupied by many things outside the teaching and learning process. Indirectly such activities may enhance the school community or facilities or culture and, as such, are worthwhile endeavours. It is the prudent juggling that school leaders and teachers do everyday to prioritise teaching and learning while building a positive school culture.

JUGGLING
STRATEGIES

- Keep the safety and education of the students as the main priorities.

- Monitor what initiatives are being introduced on top of existing practices.

- Be reflective, consultative and transparent with the school community stakeholders.

- Identify what is important, and not urgent, and dedicate time to these priorities.

- Remind all staff of the role they play in promoting the school which impacts on enrolments.

> " "

I believe I am called to be a teacher. Right now, I feel my job is being hijacked by other demands especially paperwork, compliance, student behaviour issues. Sometimes I am feeling overwhelmed. I just want to teach, that's what I love to do – teach!

Early Career Teacher

3

Delegating Roles in Schools

It has been said that people may never fully appreciate the work someone does until they leave their position. Only then colleagues may understand and appreciate their work, when gaps appear in the work patterns, because the missing person did a lot of things unbeknown to others. It is then that people have to ask whose job is it to do whatever it is that needs doing. Role descriptions and duty statements may define what the expectations are on role-holders, especially within schools. Yet there remain various and numerous tasks that may not sit within anyone's role description. Somehow, these still get done. But by whom? This chapter will unpack the role descriptions of the different staff members within a primary school and then identify the tasks that remain unassigned and discuss who should do what and how much falls back to the school leaders to do.

Here is a list of the various roles that may exist in a primary school. Please note there will be a variety of titles for similar roles, depending on the education sector and governing authority and even the specific role description.

- Principal/Headmaster/Rector
- Deputy Principal/Assistant Principal (multiple depending on size of the school and responsibilities)
  - Administration
  - Prep – 2
  - Religious Education Coordinator (in faith-based schools)

- Curriculum Leader
  - Head of Department
  - Head of Curriculum
  - Primary Learning Leaders
  - Special Education
- Literacy Coach/Mentors
- Chaplain
- Teachers
- Support staff including teacher aides/school officers
- Office staff including front counter, enrolments, finance
- Grounds staff
- Tuckshop/canteen convenor
- Uniform/bookshop convenor
- Parents
  - Parents and friends association
  - Subcommittees including sustainability, building, grants, social activities
  - School board – governance or advisory model

Reading this list of role holders within a school, it may be surprising to learn that there are still tasks and activities that occur in schools that seem to be left unallocated to one of these roles. Often school leaders fill in the gaps, as the tasks don't appear to be anyone's responsibility. How is this possible when schools have such a variety of roles? Schools are complex places with a myriad of activities within, and beyond, the core business of teaching and learning. An initial analysis of tasks will allow the distinction between them being a staff member or parent responsibility. Once that delineation is confirmed, then refining the responsibility to either school leaders, teacher or support staff will provide clarity. Alternately, assigning tasks to P&F or school board or individual parents will also provide clarity. As you may see, role descriptions are important.

I once asked my boss what were the expectations from our employing authority as to the hours primary school principals should work? His response somewhat stunned and disappointed me. Upon hindsight I shouldn't have been surprised, after all I had been a primary school principal for almost 20 years at the time I asked the question. His response ... 'we just have to work until the job is done.' Henebery (2023) in quoting the Australian Catholic University research (2023) reports that principals are 'working up to 60 hours per week, having sleepless nights and are leaving in droves.' The expectation from employing authorities may have something to do with this situation. Cranston and Ehrich (2002) report that sleeplessness is also a problem for secondary principals. Not good! Stapleton (2019) reports that teachers are significantly more stressed than the 'average' worker.

This is one of the catalysts for this analysis, as it makes me question whether the employing authorities are expecting too much of their principals or whether the role description of principals is unrealistic or whether principals are victims of their own dedication?

Let's explore each question and identify possible alternatives for looking after our school leaders while maintaining high-quality teaching and learning in our schools.

Do employing authorities expect too much of their school leaders? Undoubtedly the answer is YES. Currently school leaders are expected to be the leaders of learning along with numerous other roles and a multitude of other tasks they complete, because someone has to do it. (See Appendix One.)

Here is a brief list of the numerous roles school leaders may have to do while leading teaching and learning.

1. Teacher
2. Special needs consultant including being the Nationally Consistent Collection of Data (NCCD) expert
3. Change agent who can write strategic plans including the explicit improvement agenda
4. Workplace health and safety officer
5. Employment and human relations manager
6. Timetabler
7. Marketing strategist
8. Policy writer
9. Communications expert including social media manager
10. Building supervisor

Within these roles are various subsets of responsibilities that school leaders inevitably take on as they are competent and confident to manage tasks that may be left unallocated. Even at schools that have multiple leaders working alongside the principal, there are often tasks that the principal absorbs. Many of these tasks are loosely related to teaching and learning. Some employing authorities may see these tasks as distractions from the core business of schools. Please note this is not unique to Australia, with Wells et al. (2011) reporting similar trends in the United States.

Now just to be clear, school leaders get paid for 30hrs per week, same as teachers. Safe to say that many dedicated staff work many hours per week beyond their paid hours. IIn the Australian Catholic University's 2022 Australian Principal Occupational Health, Safety and Wellbeing Survey, school leaders reported working an average of 56.2 hours per week during term and 22.2 hours during school holidays (ACU 2023). Does this make numerous hours of weekly overtime right or acceptable? Let's think about it. This data also indicates that school leaders are being paid for approximately 50 per cent of the time they work. I wonder how many other professions would accept this. Now some people may suggest that educators get plenty of holidays every year, hence their after-hours work is a fair trade-off for their holidays. Here's a brief analysis of hours of workers and educators. Workers get paid for a 38-hour working week for 48 weeks a year which equates to 1824 hours per year. An educator gets paid for 30 hours per week for 40 weeks a year which equates to 1200 hours. According to research (ACU 2023), school leaders work, on average, 56 hours per 40 school weeks which equates to 2240 hours. Then there is the holiday work of approximately 22 hours per 8 holiday weeks which equates to 176 hours. The combined working hours total 2416 per year. This is 574 more hours than the average worker in Australia. Incredible, unsustainable and unrealistic.

Is the role description of principals impossible to uphold for mere mortals while having a personal life as well as a professional life?

Historically school leaders have worked tirelessly, above and beyond what can possibly be achieved within paid work hours. This has created an unrealistic expectation from education authorities, parents and society in general for school leaders to maintain these standards of work commitments. Using my two criteria of realistic and sustainable, I suggest we are due for a change before the increase in stress leave, sick leave and resignations from school leaders creates a pandemic of staff shortages, or dissatisfaction and declining educational standards. According to the 2022 ACU research on principal wellbeing, *The top two stressors remain sheer quantity of work and lack of time to focus on teaching and learning. They have been the top two stressors since the start of the survey in 2011. Each year, they show a mean score higher than 7.35 (on a scale of 1–10), with the highest ranked stressor, sheer quantity of work, having a mean score of 8.18 in 2022, the second highest on record.*

When anyone engages with school the criteria of realistic and sustainable can be used to assess the likelihood of commitment and success. If the request does not meet both the criteria of realistic and sustainable then I suggest that it may not be commenced without the risk of it not being seen to completion (notice I avoided the word failure).

It is currently difficult to find teachers for some primary school vacancies. Anecdotal evidence suggests that applications for principal positions are declining, and education authorities need to rethink their models of school leadership. School leaders also need to rethink what they can possibly do to maintain a personal and professional life. While school leaders continue to work as hard as they have traditionally done, education authorities and parents, staff and society will continue to expect them to try and fulfil the impossible role description.

Employing authorities often talk about looking after their school leaders by offering wellbeing programs (some of which have minimal uptake as they don't meet the needs of the leaders as wellbeing is a personal matter). If education authorities are serious about school leaders' wellbeing, then they need to introduce mechanisms to support the demands of the school leaders' role. If the work conditions looked after the employees, then we wouldn't need wellbeing programs. Remember if a leader takes time away from their work to attend a wellbeing program, and they are not replaced or covered, then while they are looking after themselves, their work piles up. This equals a dilemma!

Helpful mechanisms can include the introduction of other school roles that can assume responsibilities that school leaders may currently do. Primary school leaders would be supported if they had staff such as:

- Building supervisor
- Compliance officer

- Marketing strategist
- Employment and HR manager
- Communications expert including social media manager
- Workplace health and safety officer

Consider the time that educators could dedicate to teaching and the improvement in student learning if the aforementioned responsibilities were handled by another individual. Now there may be some education authorities who believe these roles can be dispersed across other school leaders. From my experience most school leaders including middle management, support staff and teachers are generally all busy, so sharing out these responsibilities to already busy people is unrealistic. Education authorities need to rethink what's possible and they need to rethink it now.

School leaders are expected to be the leaders of learning in their schools. Some of the tasks associated with leading learning include learning walks and talks, goal setting with ALL staff, tracking the monitoring of the assessment tools (reading, writing and maths), and managing the planning and reporting process, linked to the highly effective practices, as recommended by the likes of Sharratt and Fullan (2012). This all sounds quite manageable so long as these tasks are prioritised and school leaders have the support necessary to free up their time for their core business.

Let's explore a few of these responsibilities, and I'm quietly confident that you could certainly add to this list.

Staffing

Let's start with staffing matters that educators have to undertake ensuring schools function properly. Firstly, how do principals manage incompetent staff? In my experience I've had to work through the process to effectively dismiss a groundsman who was completely incompetent and unable to fulfil his duties. Did I get training at principal school? No. Was it my responsibility to work through that process? Yes, it was and thankfully, with the support of my supervisors from my governing authority.

Imagine having the choice and responsibility to not renew a contract of a very long-serving, dearly loved staff member. Once again, in my experience when I was appointing the best teachers for teaching vacancies for one year, and we had a choice to make as the leadership team, in retaining a dearly-loved, very experienced staff member or employing someone else and we went with someone else. This caused great heartache for the decision-makers and for the community and certainly for the teacher who was no longer employed. Was it the right decision for the school? Absolutely. Was there training for principals in how to not renew contracts of staff members? Not necessarily, yet it had to happen. The process can be taught, while the human relationships need to be juggled.

Imagine having to negotiate professional relationships between warring colleagues. If teachers who are teaching the same year level, do not get on professionally or personally and yet are expected to collaborate, to co-plan, to share resources and yet the relationship makes it virtually impossible. As a school leader it would be our responsibility to ensure that those teachers still create high-quality teaching and learning. The teachers should present a united front to their colleagues and to the families and the students, without necessarily getting on professionally. School leaders might have to intervene and remind the teachers of the code of conduct, maintaining a respectful environment that doesn't jeopardise the expected high quality of work.

Imagine you have staff who are in relationship, of a personal nature, with a parent from your school community. Your staff member may be single or divorced, as may well be the parent. How does that relationship look to staff, to families in the school, to students, to the governing authority? How do you work through those difficult conversations when a teacher's role and their integrity may be brought into question, when that relationship becomes public knowledge within the school community? The teacher may not be breaking any code of conduct from the governing authority and yet their reputation and the reputation of the other person, may be brought into question, as school communities are relatively close knit and often not great keepers of secrets. It is virtually impossible to stop the carpark gossip or even the staffroom gossip. It is therefore better to have exemplary behaviour, if possible, so there is no 'scandalous' behaviour to discuss.

One of the other great challenges that principals have to face is how to share very difficult staffing and budgetary decisions with the community. As a result of new funding and resourcing models, schools may have to reduce staffing numbers and increase fees. While the governing authority may have people in a position of knowledge to share that information, ultimately it will be the school leaders who have to share the impact of any resourcing changes with the community. Are principals trained in delivering such messages to the community? Probably not. Does it rest to the principal to do so? Absolutely. Now I do acknowledge that governing authorities may produce scripts to guide principals in delivering such messages. So how does one say to the parent body that we're going to increase school fees and we're going to reduce staff while still maintaining high levels of teaching and learning?

In some private and faith-based schools, the role of the priest or minister can be quite influential. While there are distinct delineations between the principal and priest's responsibility, some priests may overstep boundaries and try to gain more influence over the school. Negotiating the minefield of governance and authority in church schools can be a great challenge for principals. Once again principals are rarely trained in how to negotiate with priests/ministers who overstep the mark. It is probably not part of their role, yet by necessity it is. There are likely to be governing authorities that may guide the priest/principal relationship. However, the relationship relies on the cooperation and mutual respect between principal and priest. Should that relationship break down, I suggest it is better that each party focus on their respective core business, as they should be fully occupied without any professional dramas. The use of church or school property is a common topic for debate. If both parties have a philosophy of acting in the best interests of the students, then the negotiations around financial arrangements could be resolved.

The common themes of all these scenarios are relationships and their evolving nature and how to communicate change.

Pastoral Care

Let's now elaborate on issues of pastoral care. While Chapter Two briefly discussed these topics, we can now dive deeper. Pastoral care matters arguably have minimal impact on the core business of education. Conversely, pastoral care is also arguably central to the teaching and learning process, as students may find it difficult to learn if they don't receive ample love and care from teachers.

There have been occasions where some children have been reluctant to go home for fear of how their parents might respond to their behaviour at school and the subsequent outcome. And when a child says, 'I'm fearful that my parents will hurt me or hit me', then principals and teachers have to take immediate action to ensure the safety and welfare of the child. Taking children to a police station after work hours to allow the police to ensure their safety is one of the challenging parts of a teacher and principal's role. As rare as this is, I have done it and the following examples I am about to share.

Offering to visit a student's parent who is incarcerated because the other parent won't take the children for a visit is something else staff may do. If there are no other options for the school children to see their parent other than the staff member taking them, it might be up to the guidance counsellor, the principal or the deputy to visit the parent in jail with their children. Such pastoral care adds to the welfare of the child and supports both parents to maintain a relationship with their children.

Sadly, it is possible and even probable for there to be bereavements of parents, staff and students. Attending funerals for family members within your school community is common practice for school leaders and teachers. Also assisting to plan the funeral may be a gift that school leaders can offer families in the event that they don't have anywhere else to turn to and they don't know where to start. There are many options of assistance for families planning funerals, yet they may not know where to turn. Offering that support as pastoral care for the grieving families is a gift which some school staff may feel comfortable providing. As rare as this is, I have done it.

When families have young children, infants, babies, toddlers visit the school while their parents attend to educational matters of older siblings, it may be common for staff, to provide babysitting for the young siblings. Again, not everyone would feel comfortable doing this, and not everyone would see it as part of their role and yet it may happen. It may be such pastoral care that encourages families to enrol their children at your particular school. Does it impact on teaching and learning? Probably not. Does it build relationships within your community? Absolutely.

In recent years probably the greatest active pastoral care was the management of the global pandemic and the ability for alternative education programs to be provided to students as COVID-19 took hold of the world. There were many, many times that pastoral conversations and great understanding had to be displayed by teachers and school leaders, as parents had to adjust to the alternative education programs being provided by schools. This meant regular meetings and communications via various platforms such as Teams and Zoom. In some cases, it meant providing additional technological resources to students. Again, these are some of the extra demands that school leaders and teachers have tackled and managed through a very challenging time. Is it part of our role? I would suggest absolutely, and does it show great pastoral care as well as educational support for the children? Most definitely.

First Aid

Let's move on to examples of how educators may have to provide first aid in a school. Administering first aid is part and parcel of a teacher's job and yet managing a parent's reaction to their child's injury that requires first aid may not be. If a child sustains an injury that is quite distressing to look at, then it may be up to the principal, teacher, or deputy to support the parent as they come to terms with their child suffering an ugly injury.

Imagine having to provide first aid to a teacher who has collapsed onsite, potentially in front of the class of students. This is an example of why it is so important for staff to explain any of their medical conditions to their Leadership Team so that if this situation occurs, they know how to respond in a calm, effective and efficient matter. Along with caring for the staff member, the students need to be counselled through the experience.

There have been occasions where children have required hospitalisation from school and emergency medical responses. It may be appropriate that a staff member, principal, deputy or teacher travel with the child to the hospital, if the parents are unavailable. Again, this is offering pastoral support and first aid to a child who may be in some distress and yet it has to happen. The familiar face of a staff member accompanying the student may provide support for the students, the absent parents and even the paramedics. This task wouldn't be written down in a role description. It just has to happen and when things have to happen, school leaders often step up.

With students who have significant disabilities, it may be required that staff assist them with toileting. This again would be under strict protocols and supervision and some teachers might say that's beyond their role statement. Some may be reluctant to do so, which in some ways is understandable. Yet its important for students to participate and avoid missing out on opportunities, even if it means assisting with something like toileting. There may be more serious occasions, such as helping students with disabilities participate in activities. These require extensive training, as educators need to be prepared and well-equipped to handle the situation comfortably for both the student and educator. Such training has only come about in the second half of my career, last 10-15 years. Again, the question may be asked, 'Does this impact on teaching and learning?' Not necessarily. Is it important that it happens? Absolutely. Whose responsibility is it? I don't know. Yet is it the responsibility of the staff to ensure students have the opportunities to attend to the curriculum and the activities provided? Most definitely.

Imagine occasions where the parents are unable to care for their children, without some other support. Or if the parent has to go to hospital and they have to collect their child in an ambulance on the way to the hospital. School staff may supervise the student until the ambulance arrives, with the parents on board. School staff may have to communicate with the child the change in their leaving school arrangements, which may be alarming, or possibly not, if they have done such trips before.

These are all examples of some of the first aid and pastoral care activities that teachers and school leaders may undertake in the course of their work. Teachers are in a caring profession and as such many, and hopefully most, are quite comfortable providing such leadership as required.

Financial Management

The financial management of a school is a key role of school principals and yet one for which they will have received very little training. Financial management can include managing the budget and the resources. Setting and managing a budget is an important commitment as responsible stewardship is a moral and ethical process. It is advisable that principals should reflect on the current year's budget and then project forward as to how the new budget may be established. If school fees are part of the school culture, then adjusting (usually raising) fees is also an important process. Budgeting for the numerous priorities that are part of the school climate is a challenge for school leaders. Some of the dilemmas include:

- Should the school invest in staff or resources?
- Where can the school save money?
- Are the fees prohibitive for some families?
- Are families getting value for money?
- Are concessions or exemptions available for legitimate hardship cases?

- Are contracts rolled over or is due diligence necessary when reviewing existing contractors?
- Can we meet our loan repayments through school fees or other sources of income?

Principals who are frustrated accountants may thrive in managing the budget, while others may draw on the wisdom of their trusted advisors. As schools invest in projects, financial management may also mean managing significant projects on occasion worth many millions of dollars. This includes liaising with the project managers, yet the sole and the key responsibility of the principal is to get a good outcome. Do principals know how to read building plans? Possibly not. Do principals understand the language that architects and builders will use when having site meetings? Possibly not and yet whose responsibility is it to ensure we get the good outcome? The principal.

When a principal takes responsibility for a school and is charged with leading the multimillion-dollar budget, have they been given training in how to set a budget and to make adjustments according to variations in staffing or enrolment numbers? Have principals been trained in how to negotiate with external contractors about getting the best deal for their school? This could be the renewal of a maintenance contract, or a painting contract or the photocopier contract or your technician's contract. More and more schools are investing in more and more external contractors and yet that business management is still left largely to the school leadership team, hopefully with the support of finance officers and possibly business managers. If schools don't have such role holders, the principal will be responsible for undertaking such activities. So financial and capital project management is another key role for which principals have little training other than what's on the job.

Support accountants and procurement teams from the education authority's central pool are often great support for school leaders. As leaders know the school strategic priorities, and the school finance officers know the operational expenses, together they can manage the school finances with the support of relevant networks.

Public Speaking

When principals become leaders of their school, there will be an invariable degree of public speaking. Some principals enjoy public speaking, being a face and voice of their school comes naturally to them. Other principals may find it daunting to stand up in front of a huge audience and to speak confidently and competently. This part of the role is probably not negotiable. Principals must gain the skillset to be engaging and confident and competent to deliver their message in a public setting. There are occasions where principals may be called upon to speak publicly in front of the media. This could include a radio interview, television interview, or a newspaper interview. Note: media training may be provided by some education authorities, while other systems may rely on the principal accessing their own training.

Hosting important guests and following necessary protocols may also provide exciting challenges for school leaders. Imagine hosting the Prime Minister or the State Premier or the Governor-General at your school and be required to welcome them, follow protocols and have them engage with your school community. Once again, some school leaders would embrace such opportunities, while others would find it more of a stress. Rightly, or wrongly, there is little choice about these opportunities and ideally principals will learn on the job.

Imagine having to lead an ANZAC Day service attended by members of the armed forces who lived according to strict protocol. Reading at a memorial service in the presence of such dignitaries is something that school leaders once again are just expected to do. Hauseman, Pollock and Wei (2017) acknowledge that being involved in community events is important and school leaders often take part for the benefit of their school community. They also acknowledge that such events add to the complexity and workload of the principal role. There's another juggling dilemma.

Teachers also have to be competent speaking publicly. It is highly probable that teachers will be speaking in front of a group of parents beginning in the first couple of weeks of their career and continuing throughout their career. Every speaking opportunity may be seen as a chance to grow and improve. And remembering that the spoken word accounts for only 7 per cent of the total impression given by a public speaker, then how teachers and leaders present themselves is very important.

Extracurricular Leadership

Let's explore some extracurricular leadership opportunities that teachers and principals may undertake as part of their role. Principals and deputies often attend school camps and, on some occasions, may be asked to demonstrate particular activities, on high ropes course for example. This may take the principal way out of their comfort zone. While they have students' beady eyes watching them, it is important that they be able to overcome their initial reluctance. Leaders can show some leadership and instil some confidence in the students by being an example of how we can overcome our fears and step out of their comfort zone.

Prior to the global pandemic it was very common for schools to have interstate trips in Australia, particularly heading to the nation's capital, Canberra. The responsibility that is placed on the shoulders of all school staff in taking students interstate is enormous. While risk assessments may try to minimise and mitigate risks, it still bears a difficult challenge and opportunity. I hope such opportunities will be embraced by school leaders and they may not be scared off by risk assessments and paperwork and protocols and bureaucracy, just because compliance is becoming such a headache.

In faith-based schools it may be necessary for school leaders to step up and play the role of a minister, if the minister or priest is unavailable for liturgical celebrations and rituals. What makes it relevant for a principal is simply the fact that they are the school leader and in the absence of clergy it may be appropriate that the principal or the deputy principal fulfil that particular responsibility. Along similar lines it may be required for the school leaders to assist in church celebrations in the presence of the priest or minister. Once again their leadership is important and hence, I hope such opportunities would be embraced.

Workplace Health and Safety and Maintenance

There are many workplace health and safety and maintenance activities that schools just have to undertake, with or without the support of grounds staff. When grounds staff are away it may be required for the principal to lock the toilets and put the bins out. It may be required for the principal to clean the school gutters, both on the ground and on the rooves (this was before many protocols were introduced demanding that working at height procedures be introduced). They may also make sure the drains are cleaned, in the event that storms are coming. When crossing supervisors are away, leadership team members might have to step up and act as a crossing supervisor to ensure that families and students can cross the road safely. In the event of significant storms after hours, it would be common for school leaders to attend to some maintenance activities so that school can resume operations as soon as possible after the storm the next day. This could involve getting into the pool and cleaning out debris (I have done it and if I didn't do it, I am not sure who would have done it). It could mean working after hours to supervise asbestos checks. It may be required of school leaders to attend school in the middle of the night if there's been a security breach. It could be a mini security breach, just a window or door that has been left open and the security company requires a staff member to attend.

Occasions such as these often see the leaders step up so that they can look after their other staff. Their dedication and resilience is what constitutes leadership. Schools might have to negotiate maintenance issues with their neighbours, if there are common boundaries in place. There might be drainage or building issues that require the neighbours and the school to arrive at a common understanding about a suitable course of action. When schools have big public functions, such as fetes, it is wise for staff to inform the neighbours and negotiate the best way they can manage the traffic congestion around the school site for those particular occasions. If there is traffic congestion on a day-to-day basis around the school, it's important that the school principal or deputy negotiate with the neighbours to find suitable resolutions in the best interests of everybody. Of course, managing lockdowns and evacuations also often falls to the school leadership team, even with the support of workplace health and safety officers.

Managing Rehabilitation

Managing staff recovery after an injury or illness is something else that principals and deputies have to oversee. In working with a rehabilitation officer from head office, adjustments to working conditions may be necessary to ensure the employee may return to work as quickly as possible after an injury or illness. This is important for their mental and physical wellbeing, as people generally feel like they can contribute to their work in a positive way. Returning to work may take a graduated process, with the employee doing a reduced load and working up to their full load. It may mean an adjustment of their duties, which may add more work to others, often the school leaders, which in turn adds pressure. Regular check-ins with the employee are important to monitor their progress. Liaising with the rehab team for regular advice may be necessary to ensure a successful outcome for the employee. Developing a return-to-work plan may be part of the formal process to accurately record the agreed plans, often under the direction of medical practitioners. There may be employees who don't wish to 'make a fuss' and so will be reluctant to engage in such formalities of the rehabilitation process. As gracious as this is, leaders need to remind the employees that creating and maintaining a safe work environment is a priority and adjustments to conditions are there to support and protect the employee. The situation would become worse if the employee aggravated the injury or exacerbated the injury or illness by 'being brave'. If employees are reluctant to engage with the return to work process, then the matter becomes a whole lot more complicated and may need the intervention of the industrial relations team and the union to support the various parties to find a satisfactory resolution. The resolution may be one that all parties can live with and agree to follow, not necessarily like.

Rehabilitation officers may also be able to advise leaders in the management of work conditions for staff, such as appropriate use of ergonomically correct furniture, modifying their duty rosters, and dedicating close carparks for easier access. In more extreme cases, classrooms may have to be reallocated to allow easier access for physically challenged staff. If stairs are a problem, then reasonable accommodations may need to be made. Note the word 'reasonable'. This is very subjective and hence the advice from rehabilitation officers is critical as they can assess a situation with a fresh set of eyes and expertise of the process. They should also acknowledge that the relationship between school leaders and staff will guide the process to a satisfactory outcome.

As you can imagine, managing staff returning to work is a demanding exercise that can be emotionally taxing at times. Leaders have an obligation to look after their staff while also providing a consistent delivery of the curriculum for all students. A graduated return to work for an employee may appear disruptive to the students, yet it may be in the best interests of the employee. It is also the employee's right to return to work if they can fulfil the essential elements of their duties.

Performing

There are numerous activities in the life of a school whereby the teachers and school leadership team may be asked to step out of their comfort zone and perform. It's very common for schools to have a dress up day when it comes time for Book Week. Ideally teachers may partake in getting dressed up as book characters. Some schools would go as far as staff acting out a book, as the students enjoy seeing their teachers dress up as a character and act out of particular storybook. Would all teachers and principals feel comfortable doing this? No chance and yet would they do it? Hopefully. When school Trivia Night comes up, it's not uncommon for teachers and school leaders to form a table and participate. On some occasions the staff may perform an act if that is the nature of the event.

As risk assessments become the norm in schools, the opportunity for teachers and principals to engage in carnival activities that take them out of their comfort zone is becoming less common. Yet such activities are highly entertaining, such as sitting on a dunking machine. (May I recommend you wear a wetsuit if it's done in winter.) When schools have sporting carnivals, there may be the desire for teachers to participate. While this comes with an element of risk, hopefully staff are aware of their own physical limits. If there is the chance that teachers or principals can engage in a race, and it could be a fancy-dress race, then students enjoy seeing the teachers and their principals get involved and enjoy the activity as much as the students. Remember to do your risk assessment, as staff injuries have been known to occur during such activities.

Other dress up days may include crazy sock day, pyjama day or red-nose day. There are many charities that will encourage some form of dress up and if the school staff can be involved, the students are more highly motivated to get involved as well. When parents and friends associations put on social events and invite the staff to come along, there may be the occasion where the staff are expected to perform. Christmas concerts are an example of where school staff may be asked perform or be present in a fun, light hearted way.

It is important to still remember that any work function is still work for the staff, so be very cautious about how your professional reputation may be enhanced or harmed when you are performing in public. Remember that while enjoying a social drink at a work function may be accepted, any engagements with others while under the influence will be scrutinised and probably judged harshly. Extreme examples of how staff may do something fun might be something like World's Greatest Shave, where staff are invited to have their head shaved to raise money for the Cancer Council. Personally, I've done that twice and it is very humbling and very liberating. Having one's head shaved is not everyone's cup of tea yet something that some school leaders certainly feel comfortable, or at least willing to do.

Website Maintenance

The school website is often the main source of truth especially for prospective families, current families and the public. As such it is imperative that the website is kept up to date with accurate information. School policies may be found on the website, to which parents may refer to understand the school's expectations on students and families. Members of the public may be seeking enrolment processes as well as some operational information. Photos of school events are a great way to promote the school and keeping these relevant and current is important. Academic trends are also a valuable piece of data that prospective parents may like to peruse. Keeping the website fresh and enticing is important.

Animal Welfare

Here are some examples of looking after animals that teachers and principals might have to undertake. I have removed snakes from classrooms and playgrounds and relocated them into nearby bushland. I have rescued baby birds out of a street gutter that have fallen from a tree above the pick-up line, during arrival time at school. I have had to protect staff from dive bombing crows and magpies. In this instance, I could only recommend to those under attack that they wear a big broad-brimmed hat while calls were made to Workplace Health and Safety and the Department of Environment and Science. (Just as an aside, spending $300 on advice is not good economic sense.) I've had to remove various animals including lizards, cane toads and spiders that may have been slightly threatening to members of the community.

Summary Statement

School leaders need to have explicit role descriptions for all role holders within their schools. Within the role descriptions could be detailed duty statements, outlining their specific responsibilities. Coupled with these documents should be an analysis of the various activities that happen in school. This then allows the allocation and distribution of responsibilities to staff members. If there are activities that are identified as falling under no one's jurisdiction, then the activity needs to be reviewed. If it is a spontaneous event, then leaders will often respond. If it is a known and expected event, then it may be questioned and if it is to remain, then it needs to be assigned to a role holder.

I'm not sure whose role it is to attend to the variety of tasks within my school. Teachers get paid to teach and now they are asked to be on various committees. There seem to be more expectations after hours. When something new comes up at work there is inevitably a discussion about who is going to do it. For example, who will take the training session? Who will run the extra programs out of class time? Who will be the contact person for after hour activities? There seem to be never-ending tasks and limited staff to lead them.

JUGGLING STRATEGIES

- Develop explicit role descriptions for staff members to give clarity to their roles and responsibilities.

- Expect and model reflective practice to review school activities and their impact on teaching and learning.

- Assign responsibilities to relevant staff and parents, for all school events.

- Use the principles of personal and professional safety, along with personal and professional reputation when engaging in activities.

- Take measured risks.

66

Being a principal is easy. It's like riding a bike. Except the bike is on fire. You're on fire, everything is on fire. And the peddles were stolen.

Anonymous Educator

4

Mandatory and Discretionary Activities

Schools engage in numerous activities that have minimal or no impact on the teaching and learning process, and certainly minimal impact on the students' learning. In effect, there are school activities that take away time from the core business of teaching and learning. Now of course, people may suggest that schools are about more than just teaching and learning and hence, these activities can be justified as they support the other rationales for school activities. These rationales include:

- the building of community
- the increase in enrolments
- the financial viability of the schools
- community engagement and support.

These are examples of how schools can justify activities that may have minimal impact on learning outcomes.

Schools engage in a variety of activities, some of which are mandated and some of which are discretionary. Those that are mandatory are usually directly connected to the teaching and learning process, the core business of schools. The discretionary activities are often the activities that can be rationalised by supporting the additional reasons that schools engage in them, as described above.

Mandatory Activities

As explained in Chapter One the core business of schools is the teaching and learning. As such these are the mandatory activities that are expected of ALL teachers:

- Planning, using the prescribed curriculum (the Australian curriculum)
- Teaching, using the prescribed curriculum
- Assessing (correcting and marking/grading)
- Reporting (verbal and written feedback)
- Standardised testing (National Assessment Program – Literacy and Numeracy or NAPLAN in Australia)

The mandatory activities which schools have to undertake are the teaching of the prescribed Australian curriculum, the assessment and the reporting. In Australia we also have to do the National Assessment Program – Literacy and Numeracy (NAPLAN). This is mandatory as expected by the Australian government and directed through the various education authorities across the country. These same education authorities may also insist that their schools have a formal system of monitoring tools. These may provide a record of system-wide analysis of data.

There is much more that schools do to ensure the teaching and learning process is collaborative and inclusive of the parents. Communication and consultation are key elements to engage the parents in their children's learning journey. Teachers and school leaders will do all this, and more, in the 30 hours per week for which they are paid. In fact, doing all of this takes a lot longer than 30 hours per week.

Here is an interesting equation just for the exercise in valuing the education profession. Let's imagine a babysitter gets \$25/hour for keeping a child safe and entertained in the absence of their parents. If teachers have 25 children in their class for 6 hours per day and they have to keep them safe and entertained (educated) that would equate to \$3750 per day. Even if we allow 50 per cent off for a group discount, that equates to \$1875 per day. Multiply that by 200 days in a school year and teachers could be paid \$375000 per year. Now this doesn't happen. In fact, that figure is in line with the wage for principals of elite high schools, some of whom are paid more than the prime minister. We won't enter the wage debate nor the pay for performance conversation either. Just be conscious of what educators get paid and what we expect of them. We need to focus on what should we expect of our educators and ask if it is realistic and sustainable, assuming we want them to produce high-quality outcomes for all students? It is a reasonable expectation that teachers will do some work in their own time, including engaging with parents. How much is considered reasonable can be debated.

Be assured that schools do have a degree of autonomy as to how teachers plan, how they teach, how the curriculum is implemented in their own classrooms, in their own schools. There is an expectation that teachers will know the Australian curriculum. That they will have written evidence of their planning, so that schools can monitor its implementation, to ensure they are complying, in following what is mandated by education authorities. There is a suggestion that, to decrease the workload on teachers a central database of unit plans and resources could be developed by education authorities. This decreases the need for the teachers to reinvent the wheel. **A central database of planned units does exit in some educational jurisdictions.** Access to such plans does theoretically decrease the workload of teachers. However, that may be considered stifling for teachers who choose to be creative in the way they plan and deliver the curriculum.

The assessment programs that schools adopt to monitor student progress are also very much left up to education authorities, and in some cases, individual schools. Education authorities do have moderation processes by which work samples of students in the same grade level across schools are compared.

The Australian government does have the NAPLAN to understand student progress across the country and how it can be measured. It is also an attempt to improve student learning outcomes by tracking the data and making every effort to improve pedagogy, to then improve student learning outcomes. Whether or not NAPLAN has been successful since its introduction in 2008, again can be debated. Just an aside observation, if NAPLAN was a successful strategy I doubt we would need to debate its value every year and I suggest it would be part of the Australian vernacular in a similar way that, for example the Australian Tertiary Admission Rank (ATAR) or Higher School Certificate (in New South Wales – HSC) is known and accepted. NAPLAN is currently a mandatory activity that happens in Years 3, 5, 7 and 9 in all schools across the country, in the first term each year. While parents do have the option to withdraw their children from NAPLAN tests, statistically NAPLAN is participated in by the majority of students across the country and hence gives some data as a national measure of students' performance. What we also know is that some parents use NAPLAN data as a criterion for enrolling their children at a particular school. We also know that some teachers invest a lot of time and energy in preparing students for NAPLAN. Anecdotally some teachers teach to the test, so the results hopefully achieved by their students reflect favourably upon their teaching. NAPLAN is a limited tool and the data it provides should be used in conjunction with other school data including the Australian Council for Educational Research (ACER) tests in literacy and numeracy, along with the individual school's assessment tools. The combined data should be triangulated to give teachers a true measure of a student's performance and ability.

It is important that schools have a degree of autonomy while working within educational expectations from the relevant authorities. As we have a relatively transient population and families move from city to city, state to state, invariably they move schools. As such it is important families feel confident that in moving a student from school to school they are not missing out. Hence if education authorities can have very similar expectations, then students' learning is not too significantly interrupted by changing schools.

We also have numerous educational jurisdictions and authorities in Australia. This presents another level of complexity to ensure consistency of implementation and practice across schools. Just because a student attends a government school shouldn't mean they are advantaged or disadvantaged because they do not attend a private school. And yet each educational authority may have their own emphasis on pedagogy and particular programs, focusing on particular assessment techniques, making it difficult to maintain consistency. For example, a jurisdiction may embrace synthetic phonics as a tried and tested way to teach sound letter knowledge and spelling. Does one strategy get better results than the other? That depends on the data you draw upon to inform your analysis. What can be noted with a degree of certainty is that systems that allow teachers to teach with the degree of prescriptive structure, such as consistent unit plans or programs, allow the teachers more time to do what they're trying to do: implement the curriculum.

Discretionary Activities

In my 20 plus years of being a primary school principal I am yet to have a teacher say to me, 'I finished teaching all the curriculum for the calendar year and I'm looking for things to do.' Invariably teachers often say that they are struggling to fit everything in. This is the time when schools need to rationalise the activities they do, and decide between mandatory and discretionary activities. Let me give you a very simple example.

Commencing one of my appointments as a principal, I noted that the school had a tradition of having two whole school assemblies each week. That meant that the students were sitting in a hall, listening to presentations and messages and awards that were given twice a week, which would take a total of approximately one hour per week from the teaching time. Now if you do the maths, that adds up to approximately five to six hours a month, which adds up to close to a full day's teaching, dedicated to school assemblies, which could be two days a term. Over a year that's about a week and a half of teaching time dedicated to school assemblies. There is no doubt that school assemblies add to building community and celebrating students' successes when coming together as a whole school. However, these occasions can steal excessive time from the core business of teaching and learning.

When schools have a sporting program during the teaching time of a week, they have to question whether or not they have the time available to dedicate to such activities. Friday afternoon interschool sport, which some schools have traditionally engaged with, takes away an enormous amount of time. Anecdotally some students play as little as 30 minutes of sport during the three hours they are away from school for Friday afternoon sport. The hours that are dedicated and recommended by the Australian government for each subject suggest there is very little room to accommodate too many discretionary activities.

Let's continue the sports analysis of primary school activities. Many schools across the country would have swimming programs. Some primary schools do not have swimming pools which means they have to travel, usually by buses to a pool, to host their swimming lessons and carnivals. While there is no doubt of the importance of children learning to swim in Australia, there are huge question marks over whether or not children should learn to swim at school. We should ask whether this is a good activity to promote the school and what value it provides for the improvement of students' swimming or water safety. Of course, we want all children in Australia to be competent in and around water. The majority of children who learn to swim, learn to swim outside of school hours. One or multiple lessons per week for three or four weeks will not have huge impact on a child's ability to learn to swim. Now that may seem a controversial topic to suggest that schools need to review the swimming programs, however in all reality, the majority of children who learn to swim in Australia do not learn to swim at school and learn to swim in out-of-school hours.

I recently asked the curriculum leader of my school to do an analysis of all the discretionary activities that we choose to do. These are not necessarily related to the teaching-learning process yet are good community building activities or interesting activities. The analysis found that the school spent between 5-10 per cent of contact time on such activities. This adds up over the course of a week, a month, a term, a semester, and annually. See Table 3 in the following pages.

Here are some examples of discretionary activities that take significant time, time 'well spent'. The time and effort that schools put into preparing for school fetes is extraordinary. End-of-year excursions which are effectively 'fun days' under the guise of being linked to the curriculum cost time and money. The weekly sports endeavours that some schools participate in, especially for the upper grades, take enormous amount of time away from teaching and learning. Whether or not these activities are part of the Australian curriculum can be debated. Whether or not these activities add value to the students' learning can be debated.

When schools invest in having external providers offer experiences that their students may not otherwise get, they can expect some links to the curriculum but potentially minimal value to teaching and learning. Nonetheless, many school leaders may be reluctant to review these programs. Schools need to consciously review discretionary activities to maximise the core teaching and learning time for students.

Anything unrelated to planning, teaching, assessing or reporting must be questioned as to the value it adds to the teaching-learning process.

Purpose of Schools

Now this immediately brings into question what is the purpose of schools? Is it purely about teaching and learning or is it about giving children well-rounded educational experiences which may be enhanced through community building activities, through sporting programs, through cultural activities, and community engagement which they may not be able to access outside of school time. My observations would suggest that parents really enjoy and value schools being almost a one-stop-shop. Parents value knowing their children get a lot of experiences beyond the teaching-learning process at their school. Consequently, parents don't have to necessarily provide such opportunities from external providers outside of school hours. If this means a child has to be at school at 7:30 a.m. and not be picked up until 4:30 p.m. multiple times during the week, and the child has had many experiences added to their education, then some parents are quite often happy with that model of schooling.

At this point let's do an analysis of the hours that teachers are required to dedicate per subject over the course of the year.

Learning area		Hours per year over 37–40 weeks per year					35–38 wks/yr
		P–2	3–4	5–6	7–8	9	10
English		250–270	203–220	185–200	111–120	111–120	105–114
Mathematics		166–180	166–180	148–160	111–120	111–120	105–114
Science		37–40	64–70	64–70	92–100	111–120	105–114
Health & PE		74–80	74–80	74–80	74–80	74–80	70–76
Humanities & Social Science	History	18–20	37–40	37–40	46–50	46–50	43–48
	Geography	18–20	37–40	37–40	46–50	46–50	43–48
	Economics & business			18–20	18–20	46–50	43–48
	Civics & citizenship		18–20	18–20	18–20	18–20	17-19
The Arts		37–40	46–50	46–50	74–80	74–80	70–76
Languages			46–50		74–80	74–80	70–76
Technologies	Design & technology	18–20	37–40	55–60	74–80	37–40	35-38
	ICT					37–40	35-38

Table 1: Advice on time allocations

	P–2	3–4	5–6	7–8	9	10
Total percentage of allocated time (approx.)	72%	72%	79%	79%	49%[†]	49%[†]
Total percentage of unallocated time (approx.)	28%	28%	21%	21%	51%	51%

Table 2: Total percentages of time allocations

The next part of the equation is to itemise discretionary activities that schools choose to do and allocate the number of hours that schools commit on a weekly, monthly, term-by-term, annual basis.

Activity	Hours per year
Assemblies including preparation and rehearsals	40 (1 hour/week)
Sport during school hours including travel	120 (3 hours/week)
Fete including preparation and rehearsals	24 (4 days/year)
Class fun days	12 (2 days/year)
School feast days/special days	12 (2 days/year)
Charitable activity days	12 (2 days/year)
Transitions (moving around the school in between classes)	40 (12mins/day)

Table 3: Examples of discretionary activities and their possible hours per year

If schools place too much emphasis on discretionary activities, it can detract from teachers' efforts on teaching and learning. Please note that these are some examples and may not apply to every teacher, every week or every year. School leaders can add to this list from activities in their local context.

When you remove the hours dedicated to discretionary activities, you will notice that these hours exceed the expected hours that teachers should teach. With an exceeding amount of discretionary activities, teachers have to sacrifice subjects to allocate enough time for discretionary activities. Now if you're a specialist teacher, such as Music, Health and Physical Education, a language, Drama, Art, you would see it as a travesty of justice to give up your lessons in favour of possibly a discretionary cultural activity. Such activities will not be used for the teaching and learning process, even though the teachers will justify it as highly valuable. If you are a language teacher you might find it disheartening that your school chooses to lose language lessons in favour of a sporting program or sports carnivals. If you are their PE teacher and the school questions the value of weekly interschool sport or the swimming program, then you may be disappointed in rationalising the closing of such programs. You can almost be guaranteed that the subjects that have been sacrificed will not be made up in due course.

When school have visits from their line manager/supervisor, I wonder how often the school supervisors ask the principal about the music program or the sporting program or the language program or are they just interested in the literacy and numeracy program, possibly the NAPLAN result? These are questions that education authorities need to rationalise when they invest in supporting schools with the curriculum implementation. Very rarely in my career have any of my supervisors ever asked about the language program, the sporting program, the music program, or even the gifted and talented program.

Specialist Subjects

There is research to suggest that music can enhance children's mathematical concepts as well as their language development (Anglia, 2020). There is also correlation between the value of music and mathematical development (Hetland, 2001). Teachers would be hard pressed to rationalise omitting music when the research stresses the value of it.

There is no doubt that we need children to be leading fit and healthy lives. A good health and physical education program is an important element ensuring students have examples of leading healthy, physical lifestyles (Centers for Disease Control and Prevention, 2023). This is the rationale for placing importance on physical education in schools. Students who are physically healthy are capable of attending to learning, and hence grow and develop in all aspects of their schooling. A healthy body can lead to a healthy mind. A healthy mind does not necessarily lead to a healthy body.

There is no question that we live in a multicultural society and that students will be travelling the world and that cultural diversity should be embraced. Learning about other cultures and learning another language or two can only enhance a child's well-rounded education (Spence, 2022). Many schools only introduce the learning of a second language in the upper years of primary school. I would suggest the time to learn a second language is from the start of primary school, when the students are little sponges and willing to soak up all the new skills and knowledge on offer to them. The older a student is before a second language is introduced the more difficult it may become to learn.

There is evidence to suggest that approximately 10 per cent of the student population is gifted in some parts of life, and schools have an obligation to meet the needs of students at both ends of academic spectrum. It is important that the students who are gifted should be challenged and learning in an environment which gives them every opportunity to thrive (Carmody, 2018).

Education authorities may not be investing heavily in curriculum leaders in any of these areas, and so it's left up to the schools to see how they can best support the students. Options for schools include the employment of specialist teachers. This leaves the choice of specialist subjects up to the school leaders, in consultation with relevant stakeholders. Another option can be the engagement and employment of external providers to do intensive programs as either as part of the teaching time or as an outside of school hours extracurricular opportunity. If it is done in school time, then all students would participate in the year levels nominated to engage with the specialist. If it is an extracurricular option for students, then only those students who choose to participate will benefit from the experience. A third option is a variation in combining both these models. External providers could be employed for in-class activities. They may work with part of the school each term, spreading out the time across a year.

There are numerous models school leaders may explore to maximise the learning for all students. We must remember that if a subject is part of the Australian curriculum, then it is expected to be taught. Secondary schools have a little more latitude in the variety of subjects they may offer their students. Often secondary schools are only restricted by the challenge to recruit high-quality staff to teach a subject. They may also need a minimum number of students seeking a subject, to make it viable for the school to invest in it.

These examples go to highlight that many school activities are of great value and yet education authorities may not place the same emphasis or degree of support on these curriculum areas. There is also great evidence to suggest that our school leaders will have huge impact on the direction schools can take in any one of a number of areas. If the school leaders are at the top of their game, they may find ways to support all of these endeavours, while ensuring that schools do meet their mandatory teaching requirements by following the hours expected of teachers to fulfil the curriculum. There is no doubt that there are many school-based activities which add great community value and build spirit and enrich the lives of students and families and teachers. Yet they are not necessarily mandated, and hence how and what teachers choose to do and how and what school leaders choose to do, becomes part of the juggling act for all people in education.

Mandatory Compliance

The other important mandatory activities that must take place are all those associated with the compliance measures necessary for schools to meet their legal and education obligations. Schools are required to have teaching programs in place. They must meet financial obligations and governance requirements. Schools must meet their student protection training requirements and code of conduct training. Schools must also fulfil their workplace health and safety obligations to ensure the safety of students, staff, families and visitors to their site.

As the compliance obligations rest with various jurisdictions, schools may be asked to complete a variety of compliance reviews to ensure their obligations are met according to various measures. The timing of such reviews ranges from once every term to once every five years. The more frequent the reviews, the fewer the elements to be monitored. The more infrequent the reviews, the greater magnitude of their perceived importance, and the more rigorous the evidence needs to be to prove compliance. Education jurisdictions insist on these reviews as a way to monitor their school's work, and feel confident that their schools meet the standards required to be accredited as a reputable education provider. Reviews often take time and energy and have been known to lift the anxiety of the school staff. This may be caused by schools doing their core business without necessarily recording and documenting everything. Schools are being more heavily scrutinised than ever before. They must have evidence of their work. Everything from curriculum plans, to behaviour management procedures, to their complaints management register, to standard operating procedures for equipment usage. These are all examples of processes, policies, practices, protocols that schools are required to have to be compliant and hence accredited.

Education authorities are becoming more astute at assigning specific role holders to fulfil some of these compliance activities. It is common for schools now to employ workplace health and safety officers to ensure that all the requirements are fulfilled each week, each month, each term, each semester and each year. There are other role holders in the school who may fulfil training obligations for student protection or code of conduct. Ultimately the principal is responsible. They may in fact be involved in facilitating the training of such programs and they may also be well supported by guidance counsellors, deputy principals and student protection contacts. If a school were to fail in its legal and educational obligations, then the principal may be held responsible for failing to discharge their obligations adequately. How schools meet these obligations and juggle the mandatory and discretionary activities within the core business of teaching and learning needs further exploration.

Pareto Principle

When it comes to an analysis of the quantity of work between mandatory and discretionary, principals may be advised to use the Pareto principle, otherwise known as the 80/20 rule or the principle of factor sparsity. Schools know what they must do and if they aim to spend 80 per cent of their time doing the mandatory activities, those connected to the teaching and learning process, then that is time well spent. Conversely this leaves a balance of 20 per cent for the discretionary activities. School leaders should be regularly reviewing their priorities and monitoring where teachers invest their time and energy. The same theory can be applied to analysing schools' financial investments when preparing the budget. The two most important budget lines that support teaching and learning are staff wages and curriculum. Reviewing the budget would be important to check that the priorities are indicative of the importance of teaching and learning. Following the 80/20 rule may assist principals in their discernment when budgeting.

Summary Statement

There are so many demands and expectations placed on our staff by parents, by ourselves, by our governing authority, by governments. I wonder what I am expected to do and what I MUST do. I know I must ensure the Australian curriculum is being taught. There is so much more that happens in schools that take educators' time. I need to learn and understand how I manage to do what's mandated, what's important, and what are the optional extras that still add to the educational journey of students and staff.

School leaders must review the teachers' timetables to identify time spent on the mandated tasks. They can then review the discretionary activities, and engage the community for feedback on what their school values. This allows them to develop a rationale for time spent on activities and a rationale for any change in direction from historical events. School leaders must learn the history of their school and its particular traditions. Then upon understanding their school, school leaders can work with the community to identify priorities and practices that the school should continue.

Clarifying relevant jurisdictions and sharing such models with the community provides the relevant stakeholders with an understanding of where the authority for school decisions rests. Some decisions are beyond the school staff and hence the community will appreciate knowing who decides what and when and how.

JUGGLING STRATEGIES

- Practise transparency in managing financial investments and identifying spending priorities.

- Engage in frequent check-ins with mandatory compliance elements.

- Embed required practices into term or annual plans.

- Simplify the curriculum and attend to the mandatory elements.

- Withdraw and eliminate elements every time something is added from external sources.

"

We need to stop doing the things that are not related to teaching and learning.

Dr Janet Goodall

5

Balancing Priorities

The question needs to be asked: is the current model of education working, and if not, what needs to change? This leads to the next question – what is the purpose of formal education? And if the purpose is to prepare our children for the world by giving them the strong foundations in literacy and numeracy the success of the education system may be judged when the academic levels of students are compared with students elsewhere, across the country and beyond. The data from the Programme for International Student Assessment (PISA), of which Australia is one of the 79 government education department members, and the further data from the Organisation for Economic Co-operation and Development (OECD) suggest that Australia has some way to go to be a world leader in education. Pagaduan (2023) reports on the recent OECD analysis that 'there is a pressing need for serious reform in all areas of Australia's education system. The report emphasizes equity issues and teacher workforce challenges, especially in early childhood education and school classrooms. It is clear that much work needs to be done to ensure that every child has access to quality education, regardless of their background or location.'

As school leaders' primary business is to ensure high-quality teaching and learning, how do they manage all their professional responsibilities? I stress professional responsibilities are a priority, as that is their core business function. Now if school leaders wish to have a life outside work, and I suggest it is important to do so, then they need to manage work and life. A wise man, retired Executive Director of Brisbane Catholic Education David Hutton, is quoted as saying to his principals in the early 2000s that 'we should refrain from talking about work-life balance, rather we should talk about work-life integration.' David's rationale was that it is difficult to separate work from other meaningful activities in life, especially as technology has made work available 24/7.

Work-Life Balance or Work-Life Integration

The phrase *work-life balance* conjures up images that work is on one side of ledger and the rest of your life is on the other side of ledger, as in a balance beam. This would suggest that there may be hours allocated to each element of one's life in the 24-hour period. The concept of work-life balance also suggests that the two elements are not connected, that they are separate. They may be considered equal so there is a sense of balance between both. This just is not the case for educators. Technology means that educators are accessible virtually 24/7.

Therefore, the concept of work-life balance is completely unrealistic for educators, even if we consider the working hours that educators allocate, which already exceeds the average worker's working hours. Let's work on the premise that in a 24-hour period the average adult person may get between 6 and 8 hours sleep per night (and this might be optimistic). That leaves anywhere between 16 and 18 hours for the remainder of one's activities. If you work on the premise that educators are going to be at school for approximately 8 hours a day that still leaves a balance of 8 to 10 hours a day for some other activities.

It is impossible for an educator to do their job without doing a number of hours outside of their paid hours, by either extending the work hours at work, or taking work home. So, of the 16 to 18 hours a day it would be relatively safe to assume that more than 50 per cent of those hours are going to be dedicated to work which means the concept of work-life balance is taken out of the equation. And if an educator has a family and if they plan to eat, and if an educator plans to exercise or meditate, have time for their own personal wellbeing, 10 hours disappear very quickly. Remember we have 168 hours in a week and how educators use that is important for their personal and professional wellbeing (Behson, 2014). You can find numerous sources of advice about how to manage your life outside of work. The recommendations about sleep, exercise and family/personal time are consistent (Queensland Government, 2013).

Educators have been encouraged to consider the concept of **work-life integration**.

The model of work-life integration means that educators may be able to attend to some work tasks while living their best life outside of the work hours. For example, it's possible that educators could attend to some emails, while theoretically relaxing in front of the television. It could be that educators may be able to write or read while they're listening to music. As educators, particularly school leaders, are to be available 24/7 in the case of emergencies for their school, or their staff and their school families, then the concept of work-life integration means they very rarely switch off completely from 'being at work' because their job demands such a higher level of commitment and of time allocation. Now the current role descriptions for teachers and school leaders makes work-life integration more challenging, probably. Is the role description for teachers and school leaders making the job take up more time outside of work and cutting into their personal and family time more than ever before? Absolutely. As a principal with over 23 years' experience and 36 years in the education game I can certainly reflect that the number of hours and the demands placed on teachers and principals have increased exponentially in last 10 years. The actual hours required to fulfil teaching and school leadership jobs are conservatively double what they currently counted as (See, Kidson, Dicke & Marsh 2023). This would suggest that we have not yet changed the way we work to adapt to the increasing demands and expectations.

Work-Life Integration

The concept of work-life integration implies that as a school leader, you are also filling that role in your personal family time, creating the perception that you are a school leader even in public. This creates enormous pressure on teachers and school leaders, as their personal conduct and personal behaviour can always be measured against the professional standards that teachers and leaders are expected to uphold. It means that everything they do can be brought into question against the behavioural standards of their profession. Is this realistic and sustainable to think that a person must always be on their guard, must always be upholding the high standards that their profession expects? Does it allow a teacher or a school leader to 'let their hair down' and relax in a way that may be questioned by the public if it is not seeming to be upholding the high professional standards. Is it realistic to expect and accept that teachers and school leaders are public property, regardless of where they are? Their behaviour can be measured against their professional standards? This means that their conduct at social gatherings, their conduct in public, must measure against professional standards which the education jurisdiction sets. Is it possible that teachers and school leaders should be able to separate their profession from the person? Or does it mean that once a person graduates and enters the teaching profession, they lose some of their personal identity and takes on the standards of the profession?

Integrating work with life implies that the two may not be separated. This prompts the question: are educators allowed to have a difference of opinion from their employing authority? If an educator has a different philosophy, political view, moral or personal stance on a particular issue from their employing authority, their suitability for the profession could be questioned. So education authorities and the unions and governments need to be very clear about what the expectations are for educators regarding their professional conduct and their personal conduct, and if they have to be the same. When teachers sign up to enter the education profession, they may not be aware that they are becoming public property and their conduct will be under close scrutiny by students' families, colleagues and education authorities. Hence their current and past behaviour will certainly be scrutinised. It is common for parents to find teachers on social media and make judgements based on what they can see. This is a word of caution to all educators to be very prudent in their use of social media, so that their conduct cannot be questioned by society and certainly not by parents. While the concept of work-life integration certainly recognises that it is difficult for educators to separate their personal and their professional lives, it does prompt the question as to how much control does the education authority have over their employees and whether the person can be separated from the profession and vice versa?

Professional and Personal Commitments

In recent years there has been an influx of wellbeing programs introduced into schools. Now I would argue that if school authorities establish working conditions for their employees that are appropriate, then wellbeing programs are pointless. Yet in recent years there has been an increase in the demand for people to provide wellbeing programs 'to teach' teachers how to look after themselves. There has also been a recognition that the employing authority has some degree of responsibility for looking after their employees. While this might be true, teachers need to take their own personal responsibility for their wellbeing and welfare. No one forces teachers to look at emails after they leave work of an afternoon. Many teachers still attend to emails each evening after they have finished work for the day. Would most principals be attending to emails after hours each night and probably each weekend? Possibly and probably. Does the employing authority dictate this? No. It is up to the teachers and the school leaders to limit how much time they will dedicate to these practices after hours.

The challenge for the employing authorities is to ensure that the demands placed on teachers and leaders are realistic in line with the hours of duty plus 'X' percentage that they know everyone will be doing as dedicated educators. Teachers need to manage how often and when they responded to emails, so do school leaders. Occasionally the employing authority may send out an email or a text message asking for an immediate response within a very short time frame in the event of an emergency or a minor crisis. By and large it would be very rare that emails require an immediate response. Anything requiring immediate response should be provided through communication channels such as a phone call or meeting. So while technology provides us with the convenience of accessing our work 24/7, it also presents the need for individuals to manage and limit their usage of the devices so that they can have a personal life without the interference of their work dominating all of their time. When staff are on leave, they need to leave work behind for that period. The work will always be there when they return to work. Whether an educator is on a day's sick leave or six months of long service leave, they should leave work behind. I suspect that when educators, especially school leaders, are on leave they may still respond to emails, phone calls and texts. Guilty as charged! Some teachers are less likely to work many hours outside of their hours of duty, as the additional time may jeopardise their personal wellbeing. There has certainly been a paradigm shift in the last 10 years. Once upon a time teachers would volunteer their time to do extracurricular activities for the 'love of the job' and to provide students with other great opportunities. For example, teachers might have done sports coaching, run music camps in the holidays. Teachers who offer these opportunities are diminishing. And the education authorities and parents and teachers need to accept this generational change.

Being part of an education system is almost like being part of a political party, whereby you have to embrace the philosophies, practices and conduct as deemed appropriate by education authorities. This poses enormous challenges when individuals wish to behave or think in a way that is contradicting. It also suggests that the individual may have limited capacity to think for themselves and limited capacity to offer opinions to the broader community without approval from education authorities. Is this a reasonable request that can be discussed and debated?

Education is not a matter of life and death. It is about building relationships so parents and teachers can work together for children's benefit. It is about promoting the education profession to lift the profile of the educators who have one of the most important jobs in society. It is about improving practices so creative, new ideas may be discovered and trialled. Hence diversity of opinion should be welcomed by education authorities, so long as they do not harm the reputation of the organisation. Hence the organisation should welcome diversity of opinions, acknowledging that individuals will have their own views on particular topics, which may be in the public domain. Diversity of opinions may prompt reflection and review of practices, policies, procedures, protocols and may result in improvements in systems. In education terms this may result in improved practices for teachers and hence improve student learning. Without diversity of opinions, practices remain in the status quo and growth is inhibited and life stagnates. Not good! We don't want to stifle creativity. Educators understand that working for an organisation means complying with the education authority's expectations. It should also mean that professional debate and dialogue is welcomed and encouraged.

Investments at School

When schools look to invest time, energy, resources, people and capital projects into various priorities the school leaders are often charged with making these decisions, hopefully in consultation with the relevant stakeholders. The relevant stakeholders in many schools are obviously the teachers, the parents, school board, parents and friends associations and in some cases, the students. (In faith-based schools a priest, minister or parish council may also be consulted.) It is during these conversations that priorities can be identified and that school leaders can nominate where best to invest time, energy and money. With the support of school boards and parents and friends associations, it is possible that projects can be undertaken to enrich the lives of the students through investment in various projects. Now this may rely on the leadership of the school principal and leadership team to direct the stakeholders as to the priorities. Invariably the principal will bring their own personal bias to a school and identify areas of their particular interest or strengths that may enhance the educational journey for the students in their care. When a principal moves from one school to another school they may take their own professional bias to a new school and the legacy that their predecessors have left may be put on the backburner.

Educational improvements and safety of students must be the two highest priorities when investing in school projects. Beyond that, projects may enhance the facilities and aesthetics of the school environment.

Principal personal bias or interests could drive investments in camping programs or music programs or the creation of an indigenous space. These are all important yet funds may not stretch to cover all the items in the school's wishlist. Hence some prioritising needs to be done. And as the buck stops with the principal, the final decision may be influenced by personal bias. No judgement is being passed, simply stating the reality.

It takes an extraordinary leader to be able to invest in all projects that are suggested, most of which probably add value to the educational journey of most students. Again this is a juggling act that leaders have to undertake. In recent years there has been a significant push from the government to ensure that schools teach STEAM (science, technology, engineering, arts and mathematics). Of course, being highly literate in English is an absolute priority and yet acknowledging that we live in a highly technological world, teaching STEAM has lifted its profile in the last 5 to 10 years, to the point where high schools are now building STEAM buildings, with resources dedicated to those subjects. As mentioned in the previous chapter there is also no doubt that Australia needs to be giving students are solid educational foundation in the value of leading a healthy life and hence the teaching of health and physical education can never be underestimated also. Can schools do it all? Can school leaders drive all of these initiatives?

Sustainability

There is also a huge push in recent years for the introduction of sustainability programs in our schools, teaching students to know the world which they wish to live in and create, by practising good sustainable models of using resources (Mary, 2022). Schools need to be able to invest in recycling programs, saving electricity, minimising waste, and having vegetable gardens and bee hives, while minimising their paper usage (just to name a few ideas). Now is it a reality that all schools can undertake all of these programs? Probably not. My experience would suggest that sustainability programs need the energy and the commitment from some very dedicated teachers and some very dedicated parents. Often once these dedicated staff leave their schools, the programs can disappear. The sustainability programs need to be sustainable.

Associated with sustainability programs are road safety programs that explore ways for children to travel to school while minimising the amount of traffic on our roads (Education NSW 2023). Again these types of programs require huge investments of time and energy from some very dedicated individuals.

Teachers do not want additional things to be added to the curriculum. In fact, they would probably like things to be taken out of the curriculum because they are often time poor. Yet there is great evidence to suggest that all these programs add value to the teaching-learning journey of all of our students. 'How do we fit all this in?' is the question. And should the parents have some input into what the direction the school's curriculum programs can be, could be, should be? The parents are paying the school fees (for the private schools), the parents are 'the clients' and yet the teachers and education authorities may be the ones dictating the direction of the school.

Relationships, Relationships, Relationships

When I was a first-time principal in 2001, my Area Supervisor told me that my job was about 'the three Rs – Relationships, Relationships, Relationships'. Those words have held true for me for the last 20 years (or the first 20 years of my principalship career – whichever way you say it, 20 years is a few years leading schools.)

In recent years the role of principal has evolved to ensure that compliance issues are managed and that teaching and learning remain a priority. It begs the question: how can school leaders manage the core business of teaching and learning in a safe environment while building relationships with key stakeholders?

There are numerous reasons why schools, and probably many businesses, have to meet and maintain their compliance:

- Accreditation = Funding
- Workplace Health and Safety = Safe work environment
- Compliance = Regulations
- Standards = Achievements = Reputation = Enrolments (business expansion) = Income.

This now begs the second question: where do relationships fit in to this model?

Schools and education authorities (and most probably businesses) have numerous policies, protocols, procedures, frameworks, guidelines, rules, regulations – all in order to provide high-quality teaching and learning (core business in the corporate world) in a safe (compliant) environment. Does this litany allow relationships to be built and strengthened to ensure that the core business is provided in a climate and culture that values the human connections? It is a delicate balancing act to create that climate and culture. It relies on school leaders creating teams where the strengths of the individual add to the collective wisdom, allowing the school culture to be one of trust and collaboration.

Most teachers are in the teaching profession to teach; to have a positive impact on the impressionable lives of the students whom they teach. When it comes to matters of compliance, teachers may not be as dedicated to completing paperwork or following protocols as they are to providing engaging learning experiences through differentiation, making adjustments and seeing students thrive. There is the balancing act! Let me explore some real-life scenarios to see if I can clear up some muddy waters.

School leaders are expected to follow their education authority's mandated protocols. For example, staff are expected to complete mandatory training in student protection. This is a non-negotiable and teachers may not stand in front of a class until training is complete. In all reality there may be only a handful of mandatory requirements that teachers must follow to meet their obligations. However, a school leader has numerous compliance protocols to meet to support the system of schools maintaining their accreditation. Teachers are expected to maintain their professional knowledge by participating in regular professional learning, often prescribed by the education authorities. This is to ensure that teachers remain current in their practice and knowledge. In faith-based schools there are likely to be expectations to maintain their religious accreditation and currency through professional learning. Within individual schools, leaders may implement numerous procedures to ensure consistency of practice. Once again does this litany allow relationships to be built and strengthened to ensure that the core business is provided in a climate and culture that values the human connections?

When teachers plan excursions there is paperwork required to ensure the risk assessments have been completed, that buses are booked and that links to the curriculum are relevant. If all of the paperwork is NOT complete by the due date, is that enough reason to cancel the excursion? If the protocols aren't followed what are the response options for the leadership team?

When teachers are expected to have their planning visible and available and they do not meet the school's expectations, are gentle reminders enough to build relationships and keep professional expectations managed? Or after repeated reminders do the protocols outweigh the relationship and hence a teacher would be counselled and possibly be put on performance process?

When parents/carers fail to follow the carpark procedures, is there scope to allow the guidelines to be bent to maintain and build relationships or do the protocols outweigh the human connections?

When a child misbehaves and requires a significant consequence, are the protocols followed without question, or does the context and the individual impact on the action taken by the school leadership team?

When the principal expects that teachers communicate with parents in a regular and professional way and a teacher struggles to meet these requirements, does this 'failure' result in professional guidance and jeopardise staff relationships or is there a degree of latitude allowed?

At this point may I suggest **there is no easy answer. There is no 'one size fits all' solution**. What we have are some real-life examples that principals and deputies have to navigate on a regular basis. It is these types of scenarios that require experience, wisdom and a transparent rationale in order to build a culture of trust and collaboration. It is this culture that results in the balance between honouring and following protocols while appreciating the importance of relationships between all the stakeholders of the school community.

Teachers and parents and students appreciate consistency in response to issues. Teachers and parents and students appreciate transparency in processes. They appreciate clear rationales for actions, both reactive and proactive. There will be times that decisions and actions are made by the principal without a public rationale. These decisions are largely accepted when the principal has 'runs on the board' and has a solid balance in the emotional bank account of the school community.

School principals' preference may sit in either the protocol camp or the relationship camp. The advantage of working collaboratively in a leadership team, means that each member brings strengths which should ideally balance the importance of following protocols AND the importance of building relationships.

There may be a query as to why relationships are so important in an industry when teaching and learning is the core business. Here is the rationale as to why relationships are vital as we are in the business of developing good human beings.

Parents cannot provide a complete education for their children without teachers. Teachers cannot provide all opportunities for their students without parents. Parents are the first educators of their children. Six hours per day teachers stand in *loco parentis*, in place of the parents, in educating children. Hence relationships across school stakeholders are important.

Protocols are easier to follow for employees (school staff) and clients (parents and students) with a transparent rationale. And a transparent rationale builds a culture of trust and collaboration through strengthening relationships. It almost sounds like the chicken and the egg dilemma. Which comes first? Neither and both.

School leaders are required to build a culture of trust and collaboration so that they can balance building relationships so protocols can be

established and followed so that high-quality education may be provided for all students.

To build such a culture in a school, principals have to prioritise tasks to maximise teaching and learning, while building a positive community. Covey's four quadrants (see below) of time management, as explained by the Indeed Editorial Team (2022), provide a useful model to prioritise work. This is especially relevant to educators, more specifically school leaders.

The one challenge in adopting this model is the ability to adapt and pivot when the unexpected happens in school life. Such unexpected events can occur daily or they may not occur for weeks. And the magnitude of each of these events will vary from urgent/important to not urgent and not important (yet educators may feel like they should respond!). A global pandemic meant school leaders had to adapt and respond very quickly and often. Dramatic change in weather conditions may necessitate an urgent response, whereas a new version of the Australian curriculum prompts a more measured and thoughtful response. While school leaders may not draw up the quadrants when making decisions, they may use this model as a psychological filter to prioritise their work.

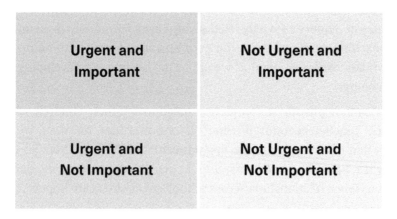

Covey's Quadrant of Time Management

Another strategy to maximise use of time by principals is the application of the Pomodoro technique. The Pomodoro technique is a time management method developed by Francesco Cirillo in the late 1980s. It suggests breaking work into intervals, approximately 25 minutes in length, separated by short breaks. Each interval is known as a pomodoro, from the Italian word for tomato, after the tomato-shaped kitchen timer Cirillo used as a university student. This strategy promotes the principal to work intensively for period of time, maximising their output then 'switching off' for a brief period. This brief period can still be productive work such as visiting a classroom for a walk-through, checking in with staff, doing a safety inspection of the playground or checking some emails. There are times when meetings will go much longer than half an hour and that's to be expected. Such meetings should be broken up with a variety of agenda items and input from various participants. The Pomodoro technique should be applied when principals need to sit and work on a project independently for a lengthy period of time.

Summary Statement

Sometimes, as educators, we have to choose between two good options, both of which add value to the teaching and learning process. There are many influencing factors to consider when determining what we should do to enhance the teaching and learning experience. We simply can't do everything, so we need to balance the priorities, somehow.

Leaders will often have to balance building relationships with the staff, students and families within the numerous protocols and practices. We understand the priorities of teaching and learning and human wellbeing, yet juggling the management of both is the challenge. Prioritising what is in the best interests of the students, coupled with what is in the best interest of the staff, while managing your own welfare can be difficult. That's the nature of being a leader in an industry that is people-centric.

JUGGLING STRATEGIES

- Use safety and educational improvements as two criteria to rationalise priorities.

- Engage all relevant stakeholders when setting priorities so there is buy in and investments in projects.

- Use Covey's quadrant of time management to analyse and prioritise work.

- Put 'out of office' on emails when on leave, whether it be for a day or a semester.

"

I bet you never learnt that in principal school.

Fr Peter Conroy (RIP)

6

Wellbeing of Educators

As discussed in Chapter Three, school leaders often work until the job gets done. This appears to be the expectation of education authorities and the community in general, suggesting that principals have to work in unsustainable conditions. What is the job of principals and school leaders? Can they possibly work seemingly endless hours, and maintain a healthy family and personal life? Stapleton (2019) reported that teachers are more stressed than the average Australian. For a profession that gets gazetted approximately 12 weeks of holidays per year and officially 30 work hours per week, this research is very concerning.

Teaching had often been promoted as family friendly due to teachers being available for their families in school holidays and after hours during the working week. No longer is this the case. Lampert et al. (2023) have suggested that the teacher shortage is directly relevant to the perception of the family-friendly nature of the education profession. Henebery (2023) has reported that principals are facing the 'perfect storm' with the combination of stressors creating challenging conditions. 'Teacher shortages are now ranked as the third biggest stressor, up from twelfth last year. On top of that, supporting the mental health and wellbeing of students [#4] and teachers [#5] means the stress of school leaders' work is escalating,' Paul Kidson from ACU (See, Kidson, Dicke & Marsh 2023).

An analysis of the data reveals that many stressors for school leaders derive from a lack of time to fulfil role requirements.

Stressors

The longitudinal sources of stress according to the ACU research from 2022 are:

1. Sheer quantity of work
2. Lack of time to focus on teaching and learning
3. Teacher shortages
4. Mental health issues of students
5. Mental health issues of staff
6. Student related issues
7. Expectations of the employer
8. Parent related issues
9. Government initiatives
10. Resourcing needs
11. Poorly performing staff
12. Complaints management
13. Critical incidents
14. Lack of autonomy and authority
15. Interpersonal conflicts
16. Financial management issues
17. Inability to get away from school and the community
18. Declining enrolments
19. Union and industrial disputes.

Researchers found the top five sources of stress to be:

1. Sheer quality of work
2. Lack of time to focus on teaching and learning
3. Teacher shortages
4. Mental health issues of students
5. Mental health issues of staff.

There needs to be a balance between the hours educators work and the hours they have for their personal wellbeing, including sleeping, eating, connecting with family and friends, exercise and meditation/spiritual reflection time (Queensland Government, 2013). It may be argued that school leaders and teachers have adequate time to fulfil their duties. While the contact hours may only be 8:30 a.m. till 3 p.m., educators are certainly expected to work in their own time and certainly some of the holidays and some of their weekends, which would be dedicated to preparation, planning and marking.

As it currently stands it could be argued that the role demanded of principals, particularly in primary schools, make the job currently unsustainable. Now what is reasonable number of hours for a primary school principal to work? That can be debated. What can't be debated is that the job is not possible to be fulfilled within the hours that principals are currently expected to work (See et al., 2023). If it is just accepted and almost expected that school leaders work until the job gets done, then it must also be accepted that teachers too will only be paid for a fraction of the time they work. The hours of duty are the hours that school leaders, and teachers, get paid for each week or fortnight. These are the hours within which the school leaders' role is described. Instead, research indicates that school leaders are working approximately twice the number of hours for which they are being paid on a week to week basis (See et al., 2023). The ACU report found that school leaders 'reported working an average of 56.2 hours per week during term, and 22.2 hours during school holidays' (See et al., 2023). How does a principal choose to spend their days when they know that they cannot possibly meet the demands of the job in its entirety? There needs to be time for educators to relax and look after themselves. Use the airline theory of supplying oxygen to oneself before you give oxygen to another person. You must look after yourself before you will be any good for anyone else (Indeed Editorial Team, 2023).

Hours to complete work

Principals may debate, discuss and argue how many hours after work they should spend processing emails, preparing reports and writing up documents. Is it reasonable and sustainable that principals do umpteen hours outside of their work hours each week so they can keep on top of the job? School leaders will work until the job is complete on a week-to-week basis regardless of our mental and physical wellbeing. The advice I was given, **work until the job gets done**, shows little regard for hours of duty. It shows little regard for a sustainable and realistic model that principals should operate within.

Green (2022) has developed a model for educators to follow to promote their personal wellbeing and minimise stress. She has developed bespoke programs for schools, explaining the rationale as to why teacher wellbeing is SO important (see Appendix Two). Wells and Klocko (2018) promoted mindfulness as one strategy to manage educators' stress. And the Australian Childhood Trauma Group (2023) provides 'practical tips and strategies to promote self-care and resilience among team members'. This proves that there is a body of research looking into the wellbeing of educators because it is of concern and in need of an overhaul.

I propose that both the employing authority AND the individual educator are both partly responsible for teacher and principal wellbeing. I also propose that it may be easier to encourage the individual to effect change in their personal and professional life to improve their wellbeing. Which may build cultural change in an organisation.

Doing an analysis of the major stressors for school leaders and identifying possible solutions may also support the notion that effecting cultural change is a huge endeavour that currently remains challenging for education authorities. For all the programs on offer and all the lip service paid to teacher and principal wellbeing, the fact that such programs are necessary indicates they are a reactive process not a preventative one. We need to treat the cause/lifestyle to prevent the stress.

Personal Wellbeing

Dare I suggest there are a couple of reasons why improving personal wellbeing is such a challenge. Firstly, personal wellbeing is just that, personal. What causes stress for one person may not be stressful for another person. How a person responds to managing their stress will vary from colleague to colleague. What minimises stress and promotes wellbeing will differ from person to person. Hence when employing authorities offer a program and have a minimal engagement rate, that may indicate the program meets the needs of just a few employees. Or alternately, employees are concerned that time to engage with wellbeing activities will take them away from their work, which will accumulate and cause more stress upon their return.

The second reason why wellbeing is such a challenge for employing authorities is that is costs money, and possibly a lot of money. For example, if the employment of a Personal Assistant (PA) for each principal in a system of 100 schools was to cost $80,000 each, that equates to $8m. Employing authorities may question what outcomes they would get from their investment. Maybe they need to do the analysis on the amount of leave that principals take as a result of stress related causes.

Back to the analysis of the major stressors for teachers and principals to identify possible preventative measures.

Workload demands and insufficient time for planning create stress for teachers and principals. Compliance, meetings and time away from the core business of teaching and learning creates stress and inhibits wellbeing. Employing authorities need to minimise the paperwork required of teachers by upskilling other staff to complete the required documentation for whatever the activity is that requires it. Teachers could also be paid to work different hours in their 'holidays' which could minimise time away from class during the teaching term.

Relationships, including the management of parent engagement and conflict, are another major stressor. One solution may be to train teachers and principals in managing such conflict. Such training must be simple and practical and dare I suggest provided by people in the profession. (I declare that I have some reservations about 'experts' in conflict resolution providing all the answers for managing school conflicts, as the culture of schools is unique. Certainly such 'experts' can provide school staff with models and strategies for managing conflicts. How about principals/school leaders who have minimal work conflicts sharing their strategies for managing conflicts. Just an idea!).

Teaching students with diverse learning needs is another major stressor for teachers and principals. Added to this is the increase in class sizes as a result of a government funding model in Australia (which is currently under review at the time of publishing), making teachers and principals work longer. Planning, teaching and reporting on more students takes more time. And differentiating for the students also takes more time. Smaller class sizes and great teacher training and professional development are necessary to promote teacher and principal wellbeing, while both strategies cost money.

Managing Stressors

Having identified some of the stressors we need to identify possible preventative measures. Remember these are generalisations, as what works for one person may or may not work for another.

Teachers and principals need to prioritise their own wellbeing and understand what works best for them in being mentally and physically healthy. It may be learning ways to say 'no' in a polite, respectful manner. This can be empowering for both the deliverer and the recipient of the message if a suggestion is made for alternative ways to get the work done.

Teachers and principals need to learn better responses to parent conflict situations or better still, learn ways to prevent the conflict. This could be to train teachers and principals in questioning techniques to build a culture of trust and collaboration between parents, teachers and principals.

Employing authorities need to invest in additional staff to complete compliance paperwork, allowing teachers to do what they are trained to do – teach – and provide high-quality learning experiences for all students.

Employing authorities and teacher unions may need to consider the model of teacher work hours and suitable financial recompense for school staff. If time is needed for planning and meetings during the work hours, then change the work hours to accommodate the same, while allowing maximum time for the teaching and learning process.

If we get the conditions for teaching right we can make wellbeing programs redundant. Imagine that!

Something must change so that teacher and leader wellbeing is not discussed because it is already managed by virtue of conditions in the workplace which make teaching energising not draining. This would result in longevity in the profession, an abundance of teachers applying for leadership, innovative curriculum development and delivery, high rates of job satisfaction, enthusiastic staff and ultimately improved student achievements.

In recent years, school leadership institutes have been established throughout Australia in recognition of the unique challenges and complexity of a principal's job. NSW School Leadership Institute Director Joanne Jarvis has reflected that strengthening principal wellbeing in turn strengthens system leadership (Henebery, 2023). This must be a general aspiration of all education systems and hence must be a priority for the authorities to lead and inspire action to affect positive change.

Work Conditions

The employing authorities must provide safe working conditions for all their workers. The fact of the matter is that the conditions under which educators are expected to work are jeopardising their wellbeing. Among the most significant burdens are the increasingly demanding requirements to record compliance evidence indicating that a school is meeting its legal and educational obligations. Amidst these compliance demands remains the expectation that teachers and leaders provide original high quality learning programs. The Grattan Institute produced a report (Oct 2022) highlighting that the demands placed on teachers to plan original units is draining many teachers, to the point where some are leaving their chosen profession. Sadly headlines such as 'Teachers hate their job' are becoming more prevalent as educators begin to question if they wish to continue working within a model that is unsustainable and unrealistic.

The rigour with which assessments are administered and data is collected is becoming unsustainable for teachers. The knowledge that teachers are required to have regarding curriculum, pedagogy, assessment, workplace health and safety, and compliance are all sucking the life out of teaching and taking the fun away from what should be an exciting, engaging and enjoyable profession. When you ask graduate teachers where they plan on being in five years' time it is not uncommon for them to be unsure with no future resolution. When employing authorities put out advertisements for leadership positions within schools, it is not uncommon for there to be a very small field of suitable applicants, or in some cases no applicants. (I was the only applicant for two positions for which I applied. The employing authority wanted more applicants and readvertised the position and approached other principals encouraging them to apply.) Employing authorities must ask themselves why they are not getting aspiring leaders to apply for jobs, and why there is such a high turnover in the teaching profession.

If two conditions cannot be met, those being **sustainability** of practice and **realistic or reasonable** conditions in which one can practise, then the conditions need to be reviewed. Now I said earlier that the individual must take some personal responsibility. Let me share a quick story with you. As a young principal I attended a meeting of principals and we were talking about workplace intensification. One of my colleagues stood up said that he had been at work every day for the past 35 days including weekends. And as an inexperienced principal I sat amongst my wise colleagues and thought to myself 'What a fool'. Why would any principal choose to be at school every day for 35 consecutive days including weekends. It was at that point that I came to the realisation that as an individual I have the right and the responsibility to say 'No'. While principals keep saying yes and rarely saying no, employing authorities will continue to increase the demands placed on them.

School leaders and teachers have a responsibility to themselves, their family and their friends to say no on occasions. If they continue to say yes or they continue to place unrealistic expectations on themselves, then their welfare, their relationships, their own health will be jeopardised. Teachers and school leaders have the responsibility to be able to respectfully say no if the conditions under which they are asked to work are not realistic, not sustainable. Teachers and school leaders often believe that they are indispensable. They may not say this yet their actions promote that belief. When I hear phrases such as 'I have to do this or I have to do that" or 'someone's expecting me to do this' or 'I've always done it this way so I must continue', that means people are not taking personal responsibility because they're responding to the demands placed upon them by others.

Let me give you some examples about what teachers may choose to do so they can set limits and maintain some degree of personal health and wellbeing. Technology is a blessing and a curse. Should teachers be setting boundaries and limits? I believe they should because without setting those limits, parents and colleagues will just expect them to respond and be disappointed if and when they don't.

Should educators be accessible via their personal mobile phones after hours. It is not uncommon at the end of the term, as school breaks up, that the employing authorities do expect to be able to contact their school leaders or representatives of the school on the school holidays. My wife believes the only way that a school principal can have a school holiday is if they travel interstate for a period of time and almost become uncontactable or at least can't visit the school. Once again this is a reflection of the demands placed on school leaders and the need for school leaders to be able to say 'no' so they can maintain their own health and wellbeing.

There will be no employing authorities who force school leaders to work 35 consecutive days onsite. There are certainly industrial relations enterprise bargaining agreements which determine the working conditions under which all employees must operate. It is important that school leaders and teachers share with their community the limitations in which they can work and operate. If I asked the question of a school leader 'Should they attend every school function?' The answer is simply No!

Should a school leader attend every extracurricular activity that their school participates in, knowing it is simply unrealistic? In a primary school that could be carnivals, musical performances, debating, after hour concerts, working bees, fete, parents and friends meetings, school board meetings, or even committee meetings. This applies to high schools as well. In fact it is probably worse in high schools where opportunities are often after hours for the students. Is it realistic that a school leader or a teacher attend all of these opportunities? 'No.' It is simply impossible and unsustainable and unrealistic to expect school leaders to attend all of those things. Hence it is imperative that teachers and school leaders say 'No.' it is imperative that teachers school leaders say enough is enough. It is imperative that teachers and school leaders set their own personal and professional limitations so that they can be healthy; so that they can be the best, most brilliant teachers and school leaders.

Sometimes 'teacher guilt' is a factor in teachers choosing to be present at every school event. This suggests that the teachers almost need the principal's permission NOT to be in attendance at some functions. There are some functions that staff are expected/encouraged to attend, especially if their students are involved. For example, a school disco run by the senior students may need teacher presence. Or the school fete when the students are performing – good for teachers to be present.

It is fascinating that educators seem to need the permission of the employing authorities or their school leaders to take ownership of the way they fulfil their work commitments, beyond the school work hours. Educators appreciate permission to manage their own work commitments. As such school leaders and education authorities need to empower teachers to take personal responsibility for their own work habits, along with offering them two strategies which will empower them to manage their work conditions.

Saying 'No'

Being able to say 'no' is an important skill that all professions need to embrace. It's important that educators have polite, respectful ways in which they can decline the invitation or request from students, colleagues or families. Phrases such as *'not yet'*, *'I can attend to that at a later date or time'*, *'can we distribute that responsibility to other people'* are empowering and liberating. These are examples of how educators may respectfully acknowledge the task requested, while they can disseminate the responsibility and the time required by handing off tasks to somebody else.

The need for school leaders to give permission to the teachers to say 'no' to various events, highlights a professional tension between giving educators their own personal responsibility for their wellbeing, while also understanding that there are certain roles and responsibilities that teachers have to fulfil. While teachers have the moral obligation to continue to meet ever student's educational needs, it is often left to the school leaders to limit and remind teachers that they have to create a sustainable and realistic model of work for themselves. As such it is important than that school leaders are proactive in setting boundaries for their teachers, so that when they do have to say 'no' it is understood and accepted by members of the community: colleagues, students and families.

This will be a cultural change for many experienced teachers who have possibly rarely said 'no' in their teaching career and the same for school leaders who have rarely done it in their leadership careers. It needs to happen so that teachers and principals can create a sustainable realistic model of work. The other important role in being able to say 'no' is the fact that this is an example to the least experienced teachers, who are entering the profession and following the example of the experienced teachers. If they see the experienced teachers attending every function and agreeing to every request, then they will probably follow suit and possibly create an unsustainable and unrealistic model for their own profession.

So experienced educators have an obligation to look after their least experienced colleagues, and set a good example by limiting what they can do, to create a sustainable work environment.

Disconnecting

The second strategy that educators should explore is the process of disconnecting from their work for certain periods of time each week. Disconnecting is a relatively new phrase that educators are starting to embrace when they limit when they will do their work after hours. It may mean that educators will disconnect between the hours of 7 p.m. and 7 a.m. every day. It may mean educators will disconnect between the hours of 7 p.m. Friday night and 3 p.m. Sunday afternoon. Again educators often feel the need for permission or at least the need to rationalise the disconnection to their employment authorities or their principals. This again is a sad reflection that educators are still yet to take personal responsibility for their wellbeing.

Our ability to work without stopping has been made possible by ever-present access to emails and work portals. Prior to these technological advances, educators never had to be concerned about disconnecting because they were less contactable. Today's educators feel it necessary to inform employing authorities that they will disconnect for a certain period of time each day or each week or each holiday, as opposed to being available and online 24/7.

Teachers need to take charge of their after-hours working conditions and manage their own work-life balance. Educators must feel free to disconnect on a reasonable limit, so that they may continue to have a life-giving profession, and not a life-draining profession. Now educators may believe that their professional union should be the voice of their profession and negotiate such conditions with employing authorities. As individuals, educators can make a decision in their personal interest. The support of unions to negotiate and formalise working conditions which are sustainable and realistic is ideal. However, if educators wait for conditions to be formalised, they may work and suffer before change is effected. If nothing gets formalised during an enterprise bargaining agreement, then educators may have to wait three to four years before another opportunity to negotiate and formalise improve working conditions arises. Hence there is great merit in educators taking personal and individual responsibility for their own actions. If this means saying 'no' and disconnecting from their profession for periods of time to enhance their personal mental wellbeing, then that's what must happen. Educators must take charge of their own wellbeing and must do it now. We want to avoid headlines like 'I'm so tired and have no time for my family' as reported by Oplatka (2017).

Management of Psychosocial Hazards

The management of psychosocial hazards (SafeWork NSW, 2021) is becoming more and more important, as workers express the need to be safe in their workplace and employers recognise the need to provide a safe work environment for everyone. This issue is relevant in all industries, from the sporting arenas to the board rooms. Everyone has the right to be safe at work, both physically and mentally. By definition, a psychosocial hazard is anything that could cause psychological harm (e.g. harm someone's mental health). Common psychosocial hazards at work include:

- Job demands
- Low job control
- Poor support
- Lack of role clarity
- Poor organisational change management
- Inadequate reward and recognition
- Poor organisational justice
- Traumatic events or material
- Remote or isolated work
- Poor physical environment
- Violence and aggression
- Bullying
- Harassment, including sexual harassment, and
- Conflict or poor workplace relationships and interactions (SafeWork Australia, 2022)

As employing authorities recognise the importance staff wellbeing, an understanding of psychosocial hazards has become part of the norm. Risk assessments maybe introduced so that school leaders are conscious of the workplace for which they are responsible and the proactive measures they may take to maximise staff wellbeing and minimise staff stress. Now documenting risk assessments is fine so long as they are enacted, reflected upon and actions taken to adjust conditions when necessary. One of the great challenges in the education sector is to accommodate the lowest common denominator, i.e., to introduce conditions that accommodate staff who are most easily stressed, while other staff may work happily and productively with greater expectations. For example, some staff will thrive in leading extracurricular activities, while others may find that expectation unrealistic. And hence school leaders can't make it mandatory for all teachers to lead such after-hours pursuits.

Think OURs, not Mine or Yours

While it is important to denote clear role descriptions and duty statements that delineate clear responsibilities, it is also wise for role holders to share the responsibilities across their portfolios when necessary. A simple strategy that can support this philosophy is shared electronic document storage. If there is a common filing system that all school leaders can access, then there is the opportunity for roles to be shared, without having the limitations of one person being responsible for a particular task. So there is a slight tension in having clear role descriptions and encouraging staff to 'stay in their lanes' while also empowering staff to work collaboratively and collegially, sharing responsibilities particularly when staff may feel time-pressured due to various activities under their management. Staff who don't have the same time pressures may be able to step in and assist when they can share the responsibilities. The electronic filing systems can be as simple as generic headings under which people will file the relevant documents accessible to the relevant people. Most teachers just need to concentrate and focus on the teaching-learning aspect of their role and not think about the budgeting or the staffing models. And while school leaders will have their distinct roles, in their absence it's important other people can pick up tasks when necessary, and hence sharing that knowledge is important to create a sustainable model of leadership.

To do this people need to shift their mindset from what is mine and yours to what is ours. World-renowned negotiator Alan Parker (1999) speaks about the importance of people shifting their mindset from working for, and as, individuals, to working for the common good. School leaders need to adapt and adopt the same philosophy so that workloads can be shared and staff can be empowered, so that the students are the beneficiaries of high-quality teaching and learning. School leaders cannot maintain their current work model if they wish to have a long career in school leadership.

Examples of where school leaders can think and work collectively is the sharing of roles across schools. Principals may find it hard to justify the expense of a full-time role in marketing, yet if a number of schools work together, the employment of one person to work across multiple schools as a marketing officer, is highly beneficial. Similarly, Workplace Health and Safety officers can also be shared across schools. This is financially beneficial as well as sharing the collective wisdom and lessons learned from multiple school environments.

Expert Opinion

When speaking at a principals' meeting in 2022, high-profile Australian psychologist Michael Carr-Gregg said that said 50 per cent of teachers suffer from anxiety; 20 per cent of teachers suffer from depression. This should be ringing alarm bells for education authorities. Three practices that improve mental and physical wellbeing are **sleep, exercise and diet**. The main sources that effect mental health for teachers include excessive workload, time pressures, behavioural challenges with students, management of bullying and reactive management strategies, difficulties with colleagues and parents. This is not new. The message is consistent from various sources. Yet minimal change seems to be occurring. Maybe you can sense my frustration – and I'm fit and healthy and managing my stress. However I am thinking about my colleagues, some of whom are in these frightening statistics.

Peta Sigley of Springfox, the workplace resilience organisation, understands the challenging times that principals face. In talking with Brett Henebery (2023), Sigley believes that when it comes to building individual and collective resilience, to manage the challenges and protect the long-term wellbeing of educators, there are some effective strategies that should be employed. Staff need to be supported and hence if they carefully **delete, delegate and prioritise work**, in order to improve efficiencies, that should prevent stress and prevent burnout. Leaders need to be **establishing trust** with staff which is critical to building psychological safety and allowing high performance to thrive. There are some basic resilience building practices that are key for all educators. **Sufficient sleep**, a **healthy nourishing diet** and **regular exercise** form the foundation of resilience. Without them people's physical and mental wellbeing can be compromised. As an expert in her field, Sigley understands these actions may be simple, yet the impact may not be underestimated. She also promotes moments of mindfulness and breathing exercises, just to slow down and to readjust perspective in our work environments.

Summary Statement

There are only so many hours in the day and I only get paid to work 30 hours per week. I know that educators have to work after hours each week and often have to work in the holidays to be prepared for the week ahead. I have a life outside of teaching and yet I feel that teaching and leading are almost all consuming. I feel like I have to respond to emails when they arrive in my inbox. I know what's important in the teaching and learning process. I need to learn how to juggle my work commitments with everything else in my life. I need to learn what hours are reasonable to work and what the consequences are if things don't get done. While I keep doing everything and working long hours, then that becomes the expectation. Is it realistic and sustainable? Educators need to be conscious of their stressors and put boundaries around their personal life so they can work to live and live to work.

Oplatka (2017) recommends strengthening school autonomy, increasing the number of positions in middle management, preparing future principals for the heavy workload, and encouraging supportive superiors who are sensitive to this issue.

Weldon and Ingvarson (2016) recommend strategies to manage the workload of both teachers and school leaders. Increasing budgets and simplifying compliance were top priorities from principals. This is consistent with ideas discussed in previous chapters.

JUGGLING STRATEGIES

- Identify wellbeing strategies that are relevant to you.

- Identify what will impact on leaders and teachers' work to promote life-giving strategies and minimise stress.

- Take personal responsibility for your wellbeing.

- Practise wellbeing strategies including sleep, diet and exercise.

- Structure professional time after hours and limit that time so personal time is maintained.

- Discern, delegate and delete responsibilities.

> "People are leaving the job or the profession because the job is ridiculously hard and not fun.

Anonymous Principal

7

Under Pressure

On a 'normal' working day I was called to attend to a teacher who had collapsed in the doorway of the classroom, in front of her students just as the first lunch break was commencing. I rushed to the room to find the teacher in a semi-conscious state, lying partially on her side, bleeding from a facial injury. I sought the assistance of other staff, an ambulance was called and we supported the teacher until the ambulance arrived. While waiting for the ambulance, the teacher regained consciousness and was able to respond to some questions to determine what had happened to the best of her knowledge. It was later revealed that the lady had a neurological condition which was not on record at the time. The result of this medical episode was a few weeks on sick leave, while a battery of tests were performed.

This is an example of where an immediate response is necessary to ensure the wellbeing of a staff member. In my career there have been similar occasions where students have had medical episodes that have required immediate attention. As a school leader, it is often left to the principal to determine what is the best course of action, as the responsibility ultimately rests with them. Now not every principal thrives under pressure and not every principal enjoys making on the spot decisions and yet they are often necessary. Are all decisions the right decisions? Potentially not. All the decisions made should be in the best interest of the student or the staff member or the family. It is important that the decisions made can be rationalised in the event that families or staff ask questions after the event. Invariably there will be paperwork to complete and often follow-up by the Workplace Health and Safety Advisors and the Rehabilitation Team. Hence accurate recording of incidents is important.

Responding to a Student's Behaviour Choice

Occasionally a student's behaviour may require an immediate response from the school leadership. If a student's poor choice warrants an immediate response, there maybe processes and protocols that should be followed to ensure that justice is seen to be done. On occasions a child may be verbally or physically aggressive to another student or staff member, prompting action from school leaders. Some schools may have staff dedicated to behaviour management, such as Guidance Counsellors. They are often called in to support student behavioural concerns. Ideally these occasions are rare yet they do exist and hence school leaders need to be prepared to model strong leadership to ensure the safety and wellbeing of all students. Formal sanctions such as suspension, or in extreme cases expulsion, may be necessary. The process of suspending a child needs to be done once a complete understanding of the context has been explained to the principal. Staff and parents need to understand that the responsibility for such decisions rests with the principal or the deputy. Schools may have a database on which they record behaviours of students. There will also be protocols that principals have to follow to ensure that the response is fair and just. Note, a communication with the student's carers/parents is also important so that they can support the decision of the school and understand the rationale for such a decision.

Parents and teachers also need to accept and understand that decisions are generally made in the best interest of all students. Now when a school leader makes a decision that appears inconsistent with earlier decisions, the need for transparency is heightened. When school leaders make decisions under pressure, they may make poor decisions on occasion. As unintentional as this would be, it still happens.

School leaders are often called upon to make decisions about the consequence for an inappropriate behaviour of a student. It may be perceived that the same behaviour from different students warrants the same consequence. This may not always be the case. I recently met with some parents who quoted to me the consequence for a child's behaviour (not their child, another child). They compared the consequence of the perpetrator who had hurt their own child. The consequence which I was responsible in issuing was different. And in the eyes of the parents, the consequences were incongruent. How is this so? they asked somewhat bewildered. Like the judicial system the punishment doesn't always appear to fit the crime. How come? Was their inquiring response. There are numerous questions that school leaders ask when issuing consequences for inappropriate student (perpetrator) behaviour.

Questions such as:

- Does the student have any medical condition?
- Does the student have a stable home life?
- Are the parents capable and willing to support the school with any sanction?
- Will the sanction have any effect in changing the student's behaviour?
- Is the consequence visible to other students, staff and families so the school is being seen to act?
- Was the behaviour intentional or spontaneous?
- Was the student in a lucid and cognitive state when acting out?

Imagine trying to make a decision under pressure while considering these questions almost immediately. How should a school leader respond? And in what timeframe could they respond? See the tips at the end of the chapter for some ideas.

Responding to Parent Complaint About Child's Treatment

What a child goes home and complains to their parents about their treatment at school, parents have got three choices in how to respond. The first choice is to believe what the child's recounted is perfectly accurate and hence contact the school immediately and express their disappointment and concern over the child's treatment. Second response from the parent may be to dismiss the child's concerns and tell them to move on with life and not worry about the school's treatment of the child. The risk with this response is that the parents may miss something important. The third response from the parents should be to listen to their child and then make enquiries at the school to understand more fully what has happened. It is the first response from the parents where they contact the school immediately and make accusations about the mistreatment of their child that may require an immediate response from the principal.

Often the principal is not able to offer an immediate response. The principal is required to listen, if they are in fact available, without necessarily providing a response at the time. It is important that the emotion can be taken out of such interactions so that both parties may deal in fact and not emotion. The parents' emotions are real and must be acknowledged. If the principal has made a decision based on information provided by the staff, the principal may in fact choose to defer a response to the parent and buy themselves some time to reflect upon the decision in the process. Time will be the principal's greatest friend when under pressure.

Responding to a Parent's Complaint Child's Progress

If a student isn't progressing as a parent would like, parents may choose to ask the school leadership team what the best course of action is to ensure the student continues to learn. The first enquiry about a child's progress should be directed to their teacher. If the parent is not satisfied, they may choose to escalate their queries to the learning support team or the deputy of the principal. This conversation about the effectiveness of the teaching is imperative so that the principal and deputy have an understanding of the data which indicates the student's progress. This data may be kept electronically or may be paper-based. Schools often have data walls which record the progress particularly of English literacy so that they can have a snapshot of the whole school's development, while pinpointing individual students' progress. These data walls may be in the principal's office where the principal has immediate access to their core business. Alternately data walls may be in a planning room where the teachers can analyse students' progress during their planning sessions.

When a parent decides to visit the school, the principal should be able to explain the school's intervention strategies. This doesn't mean that the principal has to have intimate knowledge of all the students' progress. It does mean they have to have a handle on the school's agreed effective and expected practices. It also means that the principal does have to have thorough knowledge of modern pedagogy that will have the most impact on a student's development. Teachers only want what is best for the students in their class. And while the parents and the teachers can focus on individual students' progress, strategies can be put in place to effect positive change. Parents may seek the advice of the principal as to whether or not their child needs a tutor and some extra classes after school to ensure their progress is as expected. Parents might also ask the principal and their staff whether or not their child needs further intervention from external specialists, such as a paediatrician, psychologists, occupational therapists or any other allied health experts, who can add knowledge and possibly intervention strategies to the pieces of the puzzle that is every individual student. On these occasions it is important that the principal honour and affirm the work of their own staff and if necessary, recommend external assessments that may be beyond the staff's capabilities and time.

Responding to Urgent Requests

Occasionally educational authorities will send an email to school leaders requesting a response to a particular matter within a very short period of time. For example, educational authorities may send an email asking for an audit on students with disabilities in the school within 48 hours. In response to such a request the school principal or deputy will invariably take that task on themselves or delegate to another member of the team. This requires dedicated personnel to attend to the task, complete the paperwork, have it checked by the school leaders before providing a response to the system. When such requests are received by school leaders, they are left with very little wriggle room other than to comply to the request. So, despite what is happening in the school at that particular point in time, school leaders must find a way to provide the requested information in a timely matter. This may be considered unreasonable, and hopefully education authorities are very reluctant to send out requests and do it very sparingly and rarely. When requests do appear, principals will be held accountable for providing accurate information, as requested, to comply with their authority's instructions.

Another example where schools are put under pressure to complete paperwork is when the school may be subpoenaed to provide evidence for a court case. Sadly, this is not uncommon and schools and systems are often subpoenaed, particularly around matters of family dispute, when both parties may request evidence of children's attendance, medical records from the school, academic performance of the student, along with anything which may add to the story of a child's wellbeing, welfare and education. This is another example whereby the school leaders will delegate the actual task which may be highly confidential to an administrative person who can attend to that matter. Realising that the matter will be signed off by the principal, they have to be aware of what information is being shared with the solicitors requesting such information. Hopefully the education authorities have systems in place which can check the information being forwarded on to legal parties. Such requests are again often time bound and require a prompt response from the school. The ability for principals and school leaders to respond under pressure in a calm and efficient away is often tested when such requests come via the email or their in-tray.

Staffing Decisions

It is critical for school leaders to have a transparent system when appointing staff, allowing for fair and transparent processes to be implemented. Staff who are on contracts understand that their position has a finite timeframe and hence their longevity in the school may be under threat each year until they are either reappointed to a permanent position or a different contract or when there are no job opportunities left in that school. It is not uncommon that staff can be on contracts for many years if they are filling positions of permanent staff on maternity leave or on long service leave, which are often two of the lengthiest periods of leave teachers and teacher aides can take. Enacted in December 2023, national government legislation will see many contract staff moved to being permanent within an organisation, not necessarily a particular school yet within a system of schools. That will give some certainty for those contract teachers. However, if a teacher is on contract and filled different roles each year for legitimate short-term vacancies, they may be on contract for many consecutive years. As school leaders determine which staff are most suited to particular vacancies each year, leaders are often conscious that they are playing with people's lives in so far as they are offering jobs only to some staff. As a principal I've heard stories whereby teachers say that they are the main breadwinner for the family; that they really need this job for their own personal self-esteem; that this job gives them a purpose for getting out of bed each day. I believe that many of these reasons are very true and yet as a principal I'm charged with making sure that I get the best teachers in front of the classes each and every year. While a person's personal story maybe very relevant to their need to be employed, should it be a determining factor as to whether or not they get jobs?

There are occurrences where principals appoint a new staff member with less experience, denying long-serving staff members the position, which can be a source of conflict. Of course, it does beg the question as to why a person would have filled multiple contracts if they aren't a good teacher? In all reality they may well be a good teacher. However, long-serving contract teachers may become complacent and need to be professionally renewed and challenged to continue to maintain high teaching standards. These are truly gut-wrenching decisions that school leaders have to make in order to ensure that the best teachers are in front of the students. Transparency is the principal's friend here, as staff will appreciate the rationale for the need for such decisions. This makes it mildly more palatable in understanding when appointments are made and when staff are not re-appointed.

These decisions sometimes have to be made in a very timely fashion and to some extent under pressure. It is often very easy to reappoint contract people even with due process being followed. It is also very difficult to tell long-serving contract staff that you don't have a position for them for the following year. Their colleagues on staff would be aware of who is likely to get jobs and who may not be going to get jobs. Once it has been announced, such news can often be divisive for the staff with colleagues invariably siding with particular staff members and sometimes siding with the leadership team for their preferred staff member. There are occasions where teachers take leave unexpectedly and principals have to appoint teachers to positions very quickly. Due process should be followed on all occasions, but this is not always possible if a staff member leaves a community very quickly through ill health or personal reasons. As a principal I've had those occasions whereby I've had to find a teacher literally within 48 hours to replace the staff member who would not be turning up for work the following week. Due process, while ideal, is not always possible. And while some directors in head office may suggest 'no hire is better than a bad hire', having a teacher in front of the students may take precedence, as least in the short term.

Budgeting and Balancing

School leaders are responsible for ensuring the school is financially viable. There are various sources of funding for schools including state government funding, Commonwealth government funding, school fees, grants, sponsorship, private investors. Trying to prioritise the various financial commitments that schools have to fulfil is a challenging task at the best of times. Schools that charge fees have to balance keeping their school affordable while keeping pace with increased cost of living, inflation, cost of resources, staffing increases and various other financial commitments. When a school principal has to balance the books and starts to evaluate what is and isn't affordable, the pressure may build on decisions that will influence where people's hard earned money will be spent. Any increase in school fees will impact a family's ability to afford the school. While some schools are proud of the fact that they charge high school fees and may or may not have bursaries or scholarships for families that can't afford their fees, there is also the philosophy that schools should be affordable. Families who choose a private education need to understand that there are financial commitments to support in order to ensure their children can attend the school.

Catholic schools may have a slightly different philosophy endeavouring to keep education affordable. While fees are necessary, they may also anticipate and accept a percentage of concessions and exemptions for families with financial hardships and limitations.

As government funding changes for the education sector, the debate around keeping schools affordable continues. The fairness of some schools having to charge fees while others are fully (mainly) government-funded, while others have private backing, is a great debate without any consistent answers. What is consistent is that all students deserve a high-quality education and to provide a high-quality education, schools need personnel: teaching and non-teaching staff, facilities and resources to ensure that the mandate of following the Australian curriculum can be achieved. This is why it is advantageous that school principals have trusted groups that will give them sound advice as to whether or not their fiscal management is serving the majority of those in their school. These trusted advisors could be a school board, could be the parents and friends association, could be a finance committee. It should be a group of people who have the best interests of all the learners at heart while also having some knowledge of budget and financial matters.

When the principal suggests a fee increase and the accompanying rationale behind such a suggestion, the advisory bodies must understand the implications of leaving the fees at the status quo or increasing the fees and risking the ability of some families to pay. As fees are a source of income for some schools, they go along to be the significant income component of the budget. Again when principals are budgeting for the following year, they are charged with the responsibility of prioritising what is necessary to provide high-quality teaching and learning. They need to rationalise if an investment in facilities and resources is more important than an investment in high quality teachers. Daring to rationalise whether or not investment in aesthetic improvements, which are cosmetic yet appealing to prospective families, is more important than investment in the latest technology for classrooms, which may enhance the learning for 21st century learners, is a challenge. While these decisions need to be made in a timely manner, to meet deadlines for education authorities or governance boards or finance committees, there is also the need for frugal planning to happen, often with a three-to-five-year vision in mind, so that funds can be allocated to various priorities each year.

Every time a principal changes schools and moves to a new workplace, they will approach their visual analysis of the school with a fresh set of eyes and identify priorities that others may not have seen. When a school is trying to attract students and staff, it needs to be conscious of what will appeal to the people needed to continue the mission and vision of the school. A fresh set of eyes might identify maintenance issues, aesthetic improvements, resources and facilities that need upgrading to keep pace with other local schools. Education is still a commodity and a very competitive environment. It is an area in which parents choose what's best for their children. Families are very mobile and we have a population that is quite transient. Hence families will use whatever criteria they wish to identify a school that they believe will meet their children's needs. Therefore, it is important that principals understand their community. They must understand what appeals to their clientele (families) so that when setting the budget priorities each year, it is easier to maintain and preferably enhance the teaching quality and increase school enrolments. Parents in our current day and age can look at various data sets to identify schools that they believe will meet their children's learning needs. So whatever criteria parents use, school leaders need to be conscious of the budgetary priorities so that they can maintain an appealing outlook for prospective families.

One of the unenviable debates I often have as a principal, is to whether or not to invest in personnel or resources or facilities. Hence it is important that principals have a philosophy and practice of transparency with their community. This often starts with the staff, helping them understand the rationale behind the decision-making process. Staff need to understand that certain buckets of money can only be allocated for certain types of projects. Sharing such information with staff gives them a degree of understanding as to the complexity of such decisions. It also often gives staff reasons as to why they may not want to be school leaders!

Union Pressure

There are various industrial unions that look after the rights of their employees, the teaching and non-teaching staff. Currently staff wellbeing is a hot topic and was discussed in Chapter Six. We discover the relevance of wellbeing to the role of unions when we consider that the demands faced by teachers and school leaders are often time-bound and place excessive pressure on already burdened workers. This needs to be taken into consideration when unions are negotiating improved working conditions.

There may be occasions when the principal asks teachers and non-teaching staff to attend to various matters which may push the limitations on the industrial award. For example, if a school was having to shuffle the allocation of classrooms, is it reasonable to expect that teachers would spend some time in their holidays getting their new classroom set up, or is it expected that the school, or the employing authorities, will give the teachers time during work hours to attend to such matters? Once upon a time when I was a young teacher it would be very common for both young and experienced teachers to be in their classrooms on holidays, setting up, even painting classrooms, in readiness for the start of school. No longer can this be an expected practice when our teachers can rightly say, if this is a work-related matter then should not the work be done during work hours? This is a great example of how generational change is impacting on the employment authorities' ability to provide the sort of education that parents may have had growing up. This is where principals need to revisit what is mandatory, and be committed to providing high-quality teaching and learning.

Schools that are heavily unionised may put school leaders under significant pressure when they are trying to rationalise a change. Moving the school forward in a particular direction may appear to jeopardise or at least affect some teachers' personal time and space. This is a huge juggle for all school leaders. There is no easy answer. There is a minimum standard that will be documented in any enterprise agreement for teaching and non-teaching staff in schools. Two of the more common topics that unions endeavour to monitor for their members are hours of duty and roles and responsibilities. While employing authorities may believe that employees should expect to work in their own time, including part of their holidays, unions may have a different opinion. Principals may ask staff to attend occasional work functions outside of hours. The principal may believe their request is reasonable. Hopefully the union will agree. So long as the principal doesn't step outside the boundaries in such agreements, then all should be well in such schools.

Medical Emergencies

One type of event in schools that put staff under pressure is medical emergencies. Schools invariably have first aid officers, nurses, staff who are former nurses and often called upon to offer an opinion. Should an ambulance be called to attend to a medical emergency, then there needs to be a delegated responsibility for a chosen few. Deciding whether or not to call an ambulance should rest with people in authority in my opinion. Now while all staff may be trained first aid officers, the ability to make a decision under pressure does not come naturally to everyone. I've seen occasions when an ambulance has been called to a school, which was completely unnecessary yet well-meaning. My school staff understand that the decision to call an ambulance will rest with a member of the leadership team. We do not want precious resources to be directed to non-emergency events at schools. So when well-intentioned people choose to act outside their professional boundaries, so long as the patient is looked after, then there will be little consequence for jumping outside the chain of command. However, without having due process and protocols and a chain of command in place, resources and time may be wasted. Of course, there will be occasions when leaders may be offsite and an emergency happens. A lesson in this situation is about making sure the delegated authority is given to someone who can cope with such responsibility and authority.

Critical Incidents

Major incidents in any workplace that require responses involving emergency services, lockdown, evacuations or a higher authority will require decisions under pressure by school leaders. Such occasions at school require the coordination of the school Critical Incident Management team (or its equivalent) to respond in a timely manner. The priority is the safety of all students, staff and visitors onsite. Most schools and education authorities have processes which school leaders should follow in order to be efficient in prioritising the safety of people. Keeping the relevant emergency services and education authority informed is key to the successful management of critical incidents.

This is one reason why schools practise lockdown and evacuation drills. While such practices may be an inconvenience to the teaching and learning process, the rituals are important lessons from which school leaders can learn. In the event of a critical incident that requires such a response, it's important to know that staff and students can follow the procedures.

In managing a critical incident, it is important that staff have delegated responsibilities. Often this is articulated in policies and procedures on posters that are strategically displayed to be referenced at short notice. Invariably the teachers need to look after the students and support staff while managing critical incidents. This reinforces the message from previous chapters about having role descriptions for staff so that people know what to do in times of a crisis. The leadership needed for managing such events can often determine the outcome. Making wise decisions under pressure is important. Directing staff and reminding them of their responsibilities is important. Following up with support networks is important. Debriefing after the event is important as the impact of such events on individuals and groups of people will only be known afterwards.

The legacy and impact of critical incidents can last for years in school communities. While the school must continue to attend to its core business of teaching and learning, acknowledging the impact of critical events must be respected. How people will respond to such events is unknown. Hence the support network and debriefing opportunities are important. Education authorities often have skilled personnel or external agencies that can provide such support. Employee Assistance Programs should be available to staff to provide mechanisms for support in a safe, confidential environment. The emotional impact of critical incidents on the leaders and all involved should not be under-estimated. While the adage says that, 'time heals', individual responses will vary. Although returning to regular school routines may provide a sense of normality to staff and students, the underlying response and impact can linger, simmer and fester underneath the seemingly calm persona of those involved. It is moments like these that the safe psychological environment must be reinforced so that staff know and feel they can be true to their feelings and emotions without fear of judgement.

Fingers crossed that most school leaders never have to manage a critical incident. The longer one remains in school leadership the more likely it is their leadership skills will be tested on such occasions. And even if they don't have to manage such an event, they may work in a school when such an event has left a lasting legacy and hence have to manage the after effects.

Summary Statement

In the pressure of day-to-day work, school leaders are often faced with having to make decisions very quickly. Rarely are matters that urgent that leaders need to make spontaneous decisions of great magnitude. School leaders need to have processes to rely on that allow them to make wise decisions quickly when required. There are often content experts whom principals may call upon to seek advice. If pushed for time, principals should trust themselves to make wise decisions. After all, leaders are capable of making decisions and that is expected in their roles. School leaders also often have a network of colleagues and advisors who may be a source of collective wisdom and support.

JUGGLING STRATEGIES

- Buy yourself some time by deflecting an immediate response by getting other information.

- Consult with colleagues on staff and within the education authority.

- Be transparent with rationales and processes for decisions.

- Use external agencies with expertise when necessary.

- Document processes and likely exemptions, so there is a record of decisions and processes.

- Have delegated authority for staff when leaders are away.

- Make collaborative decisions when time permits, by gathering the collective wisdom of staff.

- Breathe, as we need oxygen to feed our brain to allow us to make decisions with a clear mind.

"

Risk is the opportunity to do something new.

Dr Lee Anne Perry AM

8

When Everything Stops

On a Friday late in the month of May 2023 I was due to host a playdate for 30 families and their young children who were preparing to come to my school in the following year. This is a practice that this school has done for a number of years, initiating and welcoming new families, along with current families with young children following their older siblings. On this particular Friday we also happened to have some roof sheeting being delivered for a $5m building project that was nearing completion. As my site is shared with a training facility, there were 108 teachers turning up for a professional development day on the English curriculum. When I arrived at school, I noticed that the foreman for my building project was looking somewhat forlorn as the roof sheeting was sitting on the back of semi-trailer at the street entrance to my school. When I asked the foreman how things were going, he frowned and said 'we haven't ordered a crane to get the roof sheeting off the semi to the site, and it wasn't meant to be delivered today.' We decided on a location onsite where the roof sheeting could be delivered if they could get a crane soon. The usual school assembly was taking place as I was negotiating with the tradesmen and I also noticed that there were young families arriving for our playdate. Very conscious of my time constraints for that day, I asked the builders if the crane, which had arrived in a school entrance coming the wrong way, could delay the movement of the roof sheeting for about 20 minutes until we got families inside and the teachers arriving for the training could begin their session. This was all happening between 8:15 and 9 a.m. one Friday morning. What a way to start the last day of the working week.

I was thankful that I had a competent staff who could lead the normal school assembly, and other staff who could welcome the families to the playdate. This allowed me to work with what was probably the most crucial and critical aspect of getting the roof sheeting safely delivered in amongst people, so that the building project wouldn't stall, and so that everything else around the school could operate in relatively normal and safe circumstances. Thankfully everyone arrived safely for the playdate, the teachers arrived safely for their professional learning and the roof sheeting was safely moved off the semi-trailer into our school grounds, into a position of relative convenience for everybody.

This is an example of how I had to be multitasking in what were unusual circumstances where there was just a perfect storm of three events happening that were unrelated but all complex at on the same site at the same time. So let's explore how school leaders have to multitask very frequently in their regular work.

Multitasking

The global pandemic certainly accelerated the need for schools to be able to adapt to changing educational circumstances. School leaders were asked to pivot on multiple occasions as they were guided through the challenging times that required them to lead schools into the world of home-schooling. The principals were asked to adapt as education authorities sent out directives off on a day-to-day basis and often in a changing environment. Rules that were put in place one day could be changed in tweaked within a matter of hours or days or weeks. School leaders were asked to manage the welfare of their staff to ensure that education programs could be delivered remotely while also providing schooling for the children of essential workers, who had to come to school, all while managing the day-to-day operations of the school. Principals who had highly effective leadership teams would have deferred and deflected some the responsibilities onto their colleagues. This required a clear delineation of roles, open lines of communication, clear goal setting, while also following the instructions of the education authorities.

The ability to pivot and change directions was critical for the school leaders to build confidence within their school communities. It was important that the teachers trusted the decisions and the decision-making process, along with the families trusting the school leaders. During this time there were many lessons learnt by schools as to how best they could adjust to a changing educational climate. It was imperative that school leaders set the direction for the educational journey of the school while also setting the tone, hopefully one of calm confidence, that their school would get through the challenging times that existed in 2020–2022.

There is no doubt that school leaders were juggling many balls in the air during this particular time. There were the educational responsibilitiesand the welfare of students and staff. There was the need to follow strict protocols. The level of communication grew exponentially during those few years, as it was important to get out clear and consistent messages to staff and to the communities, so that life could continue in the new normal.

Since the global pandemic, the second round of new normal has been created. Schools are continuing to pivot as necessary to continue providing high-quality teaching and learning for all students, while maintaining the wellbeing and welfare of their staff. Please note that I have said school leaders were looking after everybody else. The question could be asked was 'who's looking after school principal?' That's an inevitable dilemma in the service industry that is education. The principals often sacrifice their own wellbeing and their own welfare to ensure a safe educational environment for everybody else.

Are You Busy?

How many times does a principal sit down at their desk have lunch at 4 p.m. and get interrupted by a staff member asking 'Are you busy?' This may be almost a daily occurrence for some school leaders as they spend their days working with their teachers and with students, and only making time for their own lunch at the end of the day when many other staff have left. Some staff might even have a track record of appearing at my door just as I'm about to consume lunch.

Multitasking is an essential skill for educators. A principal might be on playground duty and a staff member or a parent wants to have a conversation with them. The principal has to keep eyes on the students whom they are supervising, while also trying to attend to the person's need. The principal may ask 'can we delay this conversation for a few minutes until we can go and meet inside?' They may feel quietly confident that they can manage both tasks at the same time if it is not a matter of urgency and great importance. If the person seeking the attention of the principal requires significant time or is raising a matter of confidentiality, then it would be wise for the principal to defer until they can have a private conversation in the office. The challenge, of course, in having a conversation in the presence of students includes being overheard by the students, not being able to necessarily take notes or record the conversation if in fact there is a follow-up necessary. One technique that school leaders may employ is having a pen and a notepad in their pocket so that they can scribble a few ideas to recall the conversation.

A principal's desk may represent the processes by which they engage with their work. It is probable that principals will have busy work desks, filled with papers awaiting processing, computer screens with different documents, and a phone on standby to make calls. Principals should learn to prioritise different tasks, even when multitasking. An example can be when a principal's attention is diverted by a school secretary bringing documents that require immediate signing, while taking the time to understand what is being signed or contracted.

Principals invariably have to attend a multitude of meetings, including:

- Meetings with the school leadership team
- Meetings involving the learning support team to address learners' needs and creating strategies to support teachers
- Meetings involving the student protection team to ensure the careful management of the the wellbeing and welfare of students

While it may be nice to think these meetings are always a productive use of your time, there will be unnecessary interruptions disrupting the flow. Schools also have numerous students who require immediate attention, due to behavioural problems or unwarranted circumstances. Therefore, it is important that school leaders identify students who needs close supervision, which should be brought up in these meetings.

It is important that principals are able to attend to the important tasks at hand. While the ability to multitask is a great skill and one that is employed regularly by principals, the ability to attend to individual tasks is also an important skill which school leaders must develop so they can prioritise what is important.

Reading Emails

There are numerous occasions where a principal is torn between attending to work tasks or participating in staff activities. For example, when staff are undertaking professional development around the curriculum, the principal should also take advantage of this opportunity to enhance their understanding and provide ongoing feedback. Now it's very easy for principals to open their phone and attend to emails during such sessions. And while this may seem efficient, as leaders of learning they must participate as fully as possible in the training that is provided for the teaching-learning process. More and more school leaders are taking on leadership roles for particular areas such as curriculum, behaviour support and the religious life of the school in faith-based schools. So while the principal doesn't have to have intimate knowledge of the curriculum, they must have knowledge of pedagogy and practices that will impact on the teaching-learning process to support teachers and provide relevant feedback.

Even away from work it's quite common for school leaders to attempt to multitask their work and their personal time. It is important that principals be able to switch off completely and relax at home, but the demands and the pressures of the job tend to dictate that we need to multitask. Unfortunately, this does mean that principals perpetuate the integration of their work with their personal lives potentially the cost of their own wellbeing. I am not recommending multitasking at home because our families deserve us to be present, not consumed by our never-ending workload. Granted there are occasions where work will be done at home, yet I hope it doesn't have to be the norm. Apologies to all the partners out there who often 'lose' their educator partners to work even at home.

Pause

A phone call from a teacher saying a student refuses to do any work, is fixated on their computer and won't engage or comply, should prompt a response from the leadership team. If the student snarls and swears as soon as the teacher begins to insist, school leaders must intervene immediately. This requires an immediate response from the school leaders. Staff must be supported and know that when they call for help there will be a response. To this end the school secretary must know how to contact the school leaders at all times. Hence, whenever I leave my office I tell my secretaries where I am going and that I have my phone with me. And if the school leaders are all offsite, which happens occasionally, then how will the school respond to such student behaviours? The secretaries and teachers should also know the students for whom there will be an immediate response. All schools have students who cause teachers grief occasionally, yet most don't require an immediate intervention.

When school leaders intervene what are their options? Is physical restraint an option when the student starts damaging school property by kicking walls and doors? Should the teacher remove the class to another space to minimise their observations of their peer's behaviours? If the parents are not available or the student is in the care of the state, how compassionate should the school leaders be in their response and how much should they insist on respecting staff and being compliant with reasonable requests? Would the education authority have any staff available for an immediate response? Are police called? Are the carers available? Who on staff is best placed to respond to the student's meltdown? What if staff aren't trained in non-violent crisis intervention, what then? How severe should the consequences be for the behaviour if the carers can support the school sanctioned response, such as suspension? What will the re-entry process be when the student is welcomed back to school? Does the consequence severity increase with repeated offences at school?

School leaders often have plans for their work day and it is common for them to get to the end of a day and reflect that they 'have done nothing all day'. In fact the opposite is true. They may not have achieved what was planned, but their time was occupied by other priorities, some of which required an immediate response. Being responsive and being able to adapt and pivot is the sign of a good leader.

Let's unpack some occasions when everything stops for school leaders so they can respond to people's needs. These occasions are recounts of some of my experiences. They have all happened and are not extreme. They are just part of the work for a school leader. It should also be noted that my experiences are from relatively good schools in average to high socio-economic demographics. These events are not unusual. They occur in many schools across the country.

Staff Illness

A teacher who was on leave made an appointment to come and see me. She was bringing her husband, for reasons I was about to find out. After our usual pleasantries I asked what prompted the visit. Her response: 'last Friday I was diagnosed with bowel cancer'. Wow! The conversation then unfolded to discuss how and when and what's next. As a school leader my concern was for the teacher, her family, our staff who were her close colleagues. Questions ran through my mind as to how best to respond, offering support without intruding.

The trust staff place in their principal is humbling at times. What could I offer by way of practical and pastoral support? I asked the couple a few questions which guided our plans. What support do you have and do you want? Of course, the couple didn't know until after surgery when the teacher was home. The husband agreed to keep me posted and ask for assistance when necessary. (Older Australian males are notorious for not asking for help; men, please ask for help.)

What could I tell the staff? After having processed the news for the previous few days, the couple decided sharing it with colleagues and asking for prayers was a good idea. The news that one of their friends and colleagues was facing a serious medical battle immediately galvanised the staff into action. Donations were collected to purchase food vouchers, practical advice around accessing leave options was explored and guarantees of our thoughts, best wishes and prayers were all sources of comfort for the teacher, her husband and family. The good news for this teacher is that the surgery was successful and she is preparing to return to work doing relief teaching initially, before hopefully job sharing in the near future.

The same week that this teacher shared her news, I was also informed that a mother of students had suffered a stroke while holidaying interstate. This prompted a return to school for the children, earlier than expected. Desks, books, uniforms and meals were all sourced quickly in readiness for their return. The good news is that Mum is recovering well.

As things often happen in threes, the third medical story for that week was a former staff member contacting me to explain that his family was relocating back to our city for his wife's cancer treatment. He went on to ask if their children could be enrolled in our school for the duration of Mum's treatment. What assistance could we provide? Accommodation, meals, uniforms, fee exemption, books all provided a degree of comfort and normality for this family. The good news is that Mum is making good progress with her treatment.

This was a unique week where everything was put on hold to provide pastoral and practical support for these families. Students won't be able to learn if their basic needs of food, clothing, shelter and connection cannot be provided. Schools are often compassionate communities that can provide these basic essentials. It is not our core business, yet looking after people is the right thing to do.

Student Illness

I was called off a school assembly by my secretary a few years ago, in response to an apparently urgent meeting with a parent. As I invited the parent into my office I could see there were tears in his eyes. He was about to tell me an emotional story. The previous day his 12-year-old son had been sent home suffering from headaches. Having collapsed at home, he was taken to the emergency room where after some tests, they found the 12-year-old had a blood clot in his brain. The father had come to share with me the news of his son's medical condition and asked for prayers, as we were a faith-based school. My questions then evolved into what we could do to support the family and the young man. As the school principal I felt it was important to offer both pastoral and practical support from a school community that was known for offering its support for families in need.

There is no manual on how school leaders should respond to such a situation, and they may be managed in a different ways, depending on the school leader at the time. I did go and visit the 12-year-old in hospital to see how he was recovering after his surgery. Often just knowing that a community is available and willing to offer, is a source of comfort for families in times of need. This 12-year-old had his sporting future mapped out and his high school future mapped out. These had come to an abrupt end as result of this blood clot in his brain. Anything I had planned for the next few hours on the day that is father visited was put on hold. It was one of those events when everything stops.

Staff Death

One of the most traumatic events a community can face is the death of a staff member. The longer someone works at a school, there the higher the likelihood of having to deal with the death of a colleague. There is no manual on how to support the staff and the students and the families within your community when a staff member passes away. Sudden death is often more traumatic because there is no time to prepare for such an occasion. If a staff member has been ill and their death is expected, the community may have time to prepare and explain the circumstances to the relevant people. Trying to explain the change in circumstances to students of various ages is also a challenge for school leaders. In my career there have been number occasions where current staff and past staff have passed away. The practical support that one can provide is an important sign of compassion for those affected. The celebration of the person's life and the recognition of their contribution to the school is important, if in fact the family of the deceased staff member wishes for such acknowledgements. Schools should probably be led by the families of the deceased staff member. Frequently in times of such sadness people don't know what to do and who to turn to and often look for leadership. It is often the school principal or the deputy principals who can offer such guidance. While that is happening, school life should continue. Teaching and learning and providing understanding to the students is important. Leaders must juggle the need for compassionate relationships while continuing to operate school in relatively trying circumstances and creating a memory for the students. Now there is every possibility that some staff may be new to the community and not know the teacher who died very well. Often these teachers are invaluable as they can continue teaching while others grieve.

And here's the good news, school leaders don't have to have all the answers. They should know how and where to find the answers. Just like any leader when faced with a challenge, principals and deputies need to know when to lead, when to decide, when to delegate and to whom they should delegate. Now employing authorities may have protocols in place to guide a response in some circumstances, while there may be others occasions that demand an immediate response outside any guidelines.

The pastoral support can be provided by professionals trained in dealing with people facing trauma. Employee Assistance Programs provide free counselling services to employees. Such providers have the expertise to respond to a variety of personal and professional needs.

While the death of a staff member is distressing for the school community, the death of a parent of a student adds another level of complexity for school leaders. In my career I have walked this journey firstly when I was a young teacher and most recently as an experienced principal. Similar to the death of a staff member, the deceased parent will be known by some staff and families in the community. Schools are often great sources of support for these families as the school maybe a significant part of their social network.

As a principal I have been informed of the death of a parent by another parent who was close to the deceased. And then everything stops as the school goes into support mode, rallying around the family. The teachers can continue providing normal routines for the students while the school leaders and guidance counsellors unite to discern how best to support the family, only if and how they want. Well-meaning staff can offer their support beyond what is wanted and needed initially. This is where school leaders need to be prudent in communicating messages that families want. Sensitive questions and responses are an art that hopefully school leaders develop over time. Ideally, they may never have to use them.

Student Disclosure

When a student makes a disclosure that they are unsafe, school leaders need to respond immediately. Education authorities are very prudent in their policies and practices so the appropriate response can be enacted. When a student refuses to go home for fear of their parent's reaction to something that happened at school that day, staff must respond quickly and judiciously to ensure the safety of the student. Students rarely make up such accusations (although it does happen), hence the reason why school leaders must listen and follow protocols to keep the them safe.

First and foremost, school leaders must listen to the students. The students may need to be occupied and supervised by other staff while the school leaders consult with each other and their advisors. There are usually people who work for the school or the education authority who are experts in the processes to be followed. Invariably there are notes to be taken by asking open ended questions to clarify the cause of concern. There is the formal recording of the concern and the determination if it meets the threshold to report to higher authorities such as police or department of child safety or its equivalent jurisdictions in each state. When such disclosures happen, everything else stops and all relevant staff are called together to respond.

One of the dilemmas for school leaders is deciphering how much to tell the student's teachers. As disclosures are often very sensitive it may be prudent to give the teachers a general explanation of the need for extra care for the students at this time. Reminding the staff that students' wellbeing is of great importance is also wise so they know listening and responding is our responsibility and one we must take seriously.

Accusations of Bullying

Accusations of bullying at school or in any workplace for that matter are very serious. People in positions of responsibility need to act to ensure that the victims and the perpetrators are treated compassionately and fairly so that the bully ceases and that everyone may remain safe at school. It is often the parents who alert schools to the fact that bullying is occurring at school, as staff may be unaware of such occurrences.

We must remember that the definition of bullying is repeated and targeted inappropriate behaviour towards an individual or group, where there is a power differential. Bullying does exist sadly, and it is imperative that schools have policies and procedures in place to prevent, minimise and correct any bullying behaviours from the students. Accusations of bullying often get directed to the school leaders as it is a very serious matter. The leadership team must have provisions to sanction the perpetrators, correct their behaviours and ensure the safety and wellbeing of the victims.

Accusations of bullying often require an immediate response. Again this is one of those incidents at school when principals and deputies put other tasks on hold while they attend to the safety of the students who have been bullied. Every child has a right to feel safe at school and every child has a right to learn at school. If any child is being bullied then the perpetrators need to be managed so that they are not impacting on the wellbeing and education of fellow students. It is a serious matter and one in which schools pride themselves on minimising. We can all do better and school principals and deputies strive to do better each and every day.

Industrial Action

As employees are protected by industrial awards any changes to working conditions often require the scrutiny of union representatives. With every cycle of enterprise bargaining that develops a new enterprise agreement and theoretically improves the working conditions of employees, the possibility of industrial action looms large. Often union members are advised to take industrial action and strike for improved conditions. The leadership team are left with managing a staffing shortfall while union members take protected action. This is their right and ultimately this school leadership team, whether they are in a union or not, take responsibility for ensuring the safety and wellbeing of all the students while the majority of the teachers take industrial action and walk off the job. This is not ideal, however it is reality. I sometimes wonder whether or not industrial action has any impact on the decision-making process or whether it is just the union flexing their muscles to see if the education authority is listening. Regardless of the rationale for the union's involvement, industrial action will warrant an immediate response especially around the supervision of the students. While it is the employees' right to take industrial action, it is also the right, and more importantly the responsibility, of the school leaders to provide a safe environment for all students when industrial action does happen. School leaders are often given 24 to 48 hours notice to come up with a plan by which they can maintain the safety of the students while industrial action is occurring.

Capital Works

Schools that undergo capital works in the form of building projects often require the principal or delegate to be intimately involved in managing the project. Education authorities may have building supervisors for the project yet it is unlikely that they are on the ground everyday overseeing the project. Hence it is quite common for principals and deputies to be assisting the builders in making decisions prior to consultation with the foreman or site manager. There are occasions where the builders require an immediate response to a minor issue. It is often left to the principal and deputy to make a quick decision so that the building project does not stall and that progress may continue. Whatever instruction the principal may have given the builders, the architects may appreciate being in writing so there is a record of such communication. While the builders work in conjunction with the architect, and the architect documents every detail of the building project, invariably builders often want clarity about final positions of general power outlets (GPOs), about joinery or about locks or about door latches. As such the principal is often called just to confirm final decisions. Building supervision isn't part of a principal's core business yet it is important that school leaders are abreast of building happening in their school, as they are the ones who have to ensure that the teachers who will be occupying the space are happy. Once the building is complete there will be the official opening and possibly a blessing in faith-based schools. This will usually involve representatives from all levels of government, particularly if they have contributed any funding towards the project, as well as education authorities and possibly local colleagues and some of the parent community. These days are great celebrations as new buildings are often a milestone in the journey of a school. As such schools should celebrate and be proud of new facilities.

Summary Statement

There are so many priorities that school leaders juggle every day, every week and every year. Some of the choices that principals make may require an immediate response, where everything else may have to stop, in order for the more urgent matter to be addressed. Student and staff welfare along with safety must be the major criteria used to determine the urgency of a response. When a crisis occurs that requires immediate attention from the principal, teachers should be empowered to continue doing their job and leave the crisis management to others.

Leaders often become very skilled at multitasking, as attending to various tasks at once is part and parcel of the job. Having highly skilled people around the leader is important as leaders can delegate with confidence in their team.

When everything appears to stop for the school leaders, life must go on, allowing students to continue to learn and thrive.

JUGGLING STRATEGIES

- Know how to identify what is urgent and important.

- Be compassionate and pastoral in responding to staff, student and family needs.

- Tell your office staff where you are so they can find you if an immediate response is needed.

- Share with relevant staff the names of students for whom an immediate response is important to support the teachers and students.

- Know the external support agencies available to staff and families.

- Know the protocols from the education authorities in responding to a crisis.

> **"**
>
> Being a good school leader
> might be sustainable.
> Being a great school leader
> is far more difficult.

Anonymous Principal

Conclusion

Teaching is one of the most rewarding jobs people can do. To see children of all ages and abilities learn a new skill is exciting and often gives the teacher a sense of pride that they have influenced the growth and development of the students with whom they work. In the last couple of decades, the demands on teachers and school leaders have increased without any responsibilities being withdrawn from their role descriptions. The job satisfaction of educators has waned and the length of time that people remain in the profession is declining. This begs the question: are the current role descriptions for school leaders and teachers realistic, reasonable and sustainable? The current data would suggest ... NOT! Change is necessary if we, as a society, value our educators and the standards that we hope to produce from our current model of education.

I suggest that the saying 'practice makes perfect' should be modified to say 'perfect practice makes perfect.' Our current model of education is not always achieving what society expects it to achieve. While teachers keep practising, we are not getting it perfect. We need better practices to get closer to perfect. Only fools continue to do what they have always done and expect the results to be different.

There have been some changes in education in the last 35 years (the approximate career length of yours truly). Primary school teachers now get planning, preparation and correction time (PPCT) each week, often referred to as non-contact time. During this time, they often have a specialist teacher take their class while they attend to other responsibilities. This has, theoretically, decreased the amount time teachers are expected to work after hours. In reality, not so much. The increase in expectations has offset the PPCT. The introduction of specialists has also decreased the number of subjects that primary school teachers need to master so they can teach them. The downside is that the primary school generalist is being somewhat de-skilled and if they move schools, they may be asked to teach a subject that they haven't taught for many years, or worse, ever!

The amount of compliance that schools have to follow has increased the workload of school leaders, support staff and teachers. School reviews where school staff are asked to provide evidence of compliance measured against the School Improvement Tool (SIT) or any other educational jurisdiction tool are significant. This should create best practice, with schools striving to achieve the highest standard of excellence in the SIT. Best practice would have many of the compliance expectations embedded in daily, weekly and monthly practices. In reality, schools are often found wanting, as they scramble to record their practices which meet the compliance demands. Why is this so? The simple answer is that schools are complex beings, with many activities and events often distracting the staff, leaders and teachers from their core business of teaching and learning.

A supplementary question maybe: what is the purpose of education? It is certainly more than academic outcomes for students and yet that is often the most public measure of a school's greatness. Schools are also social environments that educate students and often their parents about numerous other aspects of life beyond the academics. Schools are also often community hubs that bring like-minded families together. They create a safe social environment in which people connect and support each other, all while attending to the core business of teaching and learning.

A final question worth considering is: should educators be responsible for everything that needs to be taught to educate a child, or should the parents be more proactive in their child's formal learning? If educators wish to 'have a life' and maintain their own personal health and wellbeing it is virtually impossible for them to be everything to everyone.

Change is necessary if schools are to keep pace with the modern culture of personal wellbeing, coupled with the demands of educating children. No longer are teachers willing to give their all to the education profession at the cost of their own personal wellbeing. Education in schools need to be re-imagined so students can be given the best opportunities, while their teachers can juggle all the expectations placed upon them while maintaining their own personal health. That's not too much to ask is it? More conversation and action is needed. The Stockdale Paradox is a concept about remaining optimistic and having faith in the future, while being willing to face the brutal facts of the current reality (Collins, 2001). Education has reached this point. We must act now.

Henebery (2023) reports that Malcolm Bromhead, former principal of the Australian Christian College network of schools, believes there important skills that new leaders must develop in order to have a thriving career. He lists firstly **leading by example**. He believes that the school leaders must model the behaviour and attitude they wish to see in their staff and students. This includes dedication to the school's mission, showing respect for members of the school community and acting ethically while striving for excellence. Leaders should also pursue their own professional and personal development which creates a culture of lifelong learning.

The second skill he recommends is **providing staff leadership and development**. A successful school leader will build and maintain competent motivated staff. This involves hiring effectively, providing ongoing professional development opportunities, and creating a culture where everyone feels valued. This then creates a culture of trust and collaboration, which is important for leadership and development.

The third skill he recommends is **building a learning community**. School leaders are the leaders of learning and hence must foster an environment where everybody feels part of a supportive community that promotes learning as the core business. This involves open communication, collaborative decision-making and prioritising students' learning and wellbeing.

Maximising learning is the next skill that leaders need. As I have repeatedly said, teaching and learning is our core business and hence we must maximise learning for all students. We must have high academic standards, ensuring that students have access to the latest resources, high-quality teachers and facilities.

Finally, effective school leaders must **nurture relationships**. As I've mentioned earlier, when I was appointed principal over 23 years ago, my boss said our job was about relationships, relationships, relationships. School leaders must prioritise building relationships with all members of the school community: staff, students and families. Again, this creates a cultural of trust and collaboration, which increases engagement, leads to a more positive school culture and improves outcomes for students.

According to Bromhead, developing these skills is a challenging process, one that we may never finish yet one we must strive to achieve. There is no doubt that leading a school can be a lonely profession. However, most school leaders go into to the profession with the right intent, the right motivation and the right aspirations to make a positive difference for the students with whom that are working. Most school leaders work with the intent of creating a learning environment where the students are the beneficiaries of the dedicated work of staff and families, so that we can create a better future for the students and each other.

Bromhead's summary encapsulates five broad themes that I have covered the end of every chapter. I've given specific strategies about what school leaders, and aspiring leaders, can do to ensure their own personal health and wellbeing, while creating a thriving learning environment. Principals need to identify their own specific strategies to ensure that learning and wellbeing are at the forefront of education.

References

Anglia, N. (2020, July 6). *The Importance of Music in Education*. Nord Anglia Education. https://www.nordangliaeducation.com/news/2020/07/06/the-importance-of-music-in-education

Australian Institute for Teaching and School Leadership Limited. (2014). *Australian Professional Standard for Principals and the Leadership Profiles*. Australian Institute for Teaching and School Leadership. https://www.aitsl.edu.au/research/spotlights/wellbeing-in-australian-schools

Australian Institute for Teaching and School Leadership Limited. (2022, March). *Wellbeing in Australian Schools*. Australian Institute for Teaching and School Leadership. https://www.aitsl.edu.au/research/spotlights/wellbeing-in-australian-schools

Barrett, H. (2017, September 5). Plan for five careers in a lifetime. *Financial Times*. https://www.ft.com/content/0151d2fe-868a-11e7-8bb1-5ba57d47eff7

Behson, S. (2014, August 1). Relax, You Have 168 Hours This Week. *Harvard Business Review*. https://hbr.org/2014/08/relax-you-have-168-hours-this-week

Beyond Blue (n.d.) Staff Wellbeing – Be You. https://beyou.edu.au/fact-sheets/wellbeing/staff-wellbeing

Carmody, R. (2018, October 22). How to tell if you've got a gifted and talented child, and what to do about it. *ABC News*. https://www.abc.net.au/news/2018-10-22/how-to-tell-if-you-have-a-gifted-child-explainer/10393244

Centers for Disease Control and Prevention. (2023, June 30). *How much physical activity do children need?* https://www.cdc.gov/physicalactivity/basics/children/index.htm

Collins, J. (2001). *Good to Great: Why Some Companies Make the Leap and Others Don't*. Random House UK.

Cranston, N., & Ehrich, L. C. (2002). 'Overcoming Sleeplessness': Role and Workload of Secondary School Principals in Queensland. *Leading and Managing, 8*(1), 17–35.

Day, C. (2007). What Being a Successful Principal Really Means: An International Perspective. *Educational Leadership and Administration: Teaching and Program Development, 19*, 13–24.

Diocese of Rockhampton Principals Role Description.

Green, A. (2022). *Teacher Wellbeing: A Real Conversation for Teachers and Leaders*. Amba Press.

Hattie, J. (2011). *Visible Learning for Teachers: Maximizing Impact on Learning*. Taylor and Francis Ltd.

Hauseman, D. C., Pollock, K., & Wang, F. (2017). Inconvenient, but Essential: Impact and Influence of School-Community Involvement on Principals' Work and Workload. *School Community Journal, 27*(1), 83–105.

Henebery, B. (2023, March 21). 60-hour weeks and sleepless nights – *Why Australia's principals are leaving in droves*. The Educator. https://www.theeducatoronline.com/k12/news/60hour-weeks-and-sleepless-nights--why-australias-principals-are-leaving-in-droves/282189

Henebery, B. (2023, April 28). *Principal profession facing 'perfect storm,' expert warns*. The Educator. https://www.theeducatoronline.com/k12/news/principal-profession-facing-perfect-storm-expert-warns/282379

Henebery, B. (2023, April 28). *Workloads slashed for NSW Teachers*. The Educator. https://www.theeducatoronline.com/k12/news/workloads-slashed-for-nsw-teachers/282378

Henebery, B. (2023, July 21). *How resilience can help principals bounce back from burnout*. The Educator. https://www.theeducatoronline.com/k12/news/how-resilience-can-help-principals-bounce-back-from-burnout/282892

Henebery, B. (2023, July 26). *Program combats 'lonely at the top' mentality for principals*. The Educator. https://www.theeducatoronline.com/k12/news/program-combats-lonely-at-the-top-mentality-for-principals/282922

Henebery, B. (2023, August 15). Why *the future is bright for new principles in NSW*. The Educator. https://www.theeducatoronline.com/k12/news/why-the-future-is-bright-for-new-principals-in-nsw/283046

Hetland, L. & Winner, E. (2001). The Arts and Academic Achievement: What the Evidence Shows. *The Journal of Aesthetic Education, 102*(5), 3–6. https://doi.org/10.1080/10632910109600008

Indeed Editorial Team. (2022, July 22). *The Covey Time Management Matrix Explained*. Indeed. https://www.indeed.com/career-advice/career-development/covey-time-management-matrix

Indeed Editorial Team. (2023, September 1). *How To Relax After Work: 12 Ways to De-Stress*. Indeed. https://www.indeed.com/career-advice/career-development/how-to-relax-after-work

KU Online Education Graduate Programs Blog. (2023, December 8). Teacher to Principal – How to Become a Principal. https://educationonline.ku.edu/community/teacher-to-principal

Lampert, J., McPherson, A., & Burnett, B. (2023, May 1). Teachers shortages: is teaching family friendly now? *AARE Blog*. https://blog.aare.edu.au/teacher-shortages-is-teaching-family-friendly-now/

Laudeman, J. (2021, July 26). Why STEAM Education Is So Important Today. *Institute for Educational Advancement Blog*. https://educationaladvancement.org/blog-why-steam-education-is-so-important-today/

Mary. (2022, October 22). *The Importance of Teaching Sustainability in Schools*. Go Greenva. https://www.gogreenva.org/the-importance-of-teaching-sustainability-in-schools/

Oplatka, I. (2017). 'I'm So Tired and Have No Time for My Family': The Consequences of Heavy Workload in Principalship. *International Studies in Educational Administration, 45*(2), 21–41.

Oplatka, I. (2017). Principal workload: Components, determinants and coping strategies in an era of standardization and accountability. *Journal of Educational Administration, 55*(5), 552–568. https://doi.org/10.1108/JEA-06-2016-0071

Parker, A., & Stumm, S. (1999). *The Negotiator's Toolkit*. Peak Performance Development.

Pagaduan, M. (2023). OECD Education Report delivers harsh wake-up call for Australia. Retrieved from https://www.theeducatoronline.com/k12/news/oecd-education-report-delivers-harsh-wakeup-call-for-australia/282311

Queensland Department of Education. (2023). *Functional job requirements for the position of principal.* https://education.qld.gov.au/initiativesstrategies/Documents/functional-job-requirements-position-principal.pdf

Queensland Government. (2013). Work/life balance and stress management. https://www.qld.gov.au/health/mental-health/lifestyle

SafeWork Australia. (2022). Code of Practice: Managing psychosocial hazards at work. https://www.safeworkaustralia.gov.au/safety-topic/managing-health-and-safety/mental-health/psychosocial-hazards

SafeWork NSW. (2021). Code of Practice: Managing Psychosocial Hazards at Work. https://www.safework.nsw.gov.au/__data/assets/pdf_file/0004/983353/Code-of-Practice_Managing-psychosocial-hazards.pdf

See, S. M., Kidson, P., Dicke, T., & Marsh, H. (2023). *The Australian Principal Occupational Health, Safety and Wellbeing Survey 2022 Data.* Institute for Positive Psychology and Education, Australian Catholic University. https://www.healthandwellbeing.org/reports/AU/2022_ACU_Principals_HWB_Final_Report.pdf

Sharratt, L., & Fullan, M. (2012). *Putting FACES on the Data: What Great Leaders Do.* Corwin Press.

Spence, C. (2022, April 29). How learning a new language changes your brain. *World of Better Learning* by Cambridge University Press. https://www.cambridge.org/elt/blog/2022/04/29/learning-language-changes-your-brain/

Stapleton, P. (2019, June 7). Teachers are more depressed and anxious than the average Australian. SBS News. https://www.sbs.com.au/news/insight/article/teachers-are-more-depressed-and-anxious-than-the-average-australian/attutptyz

The ACT Group. (2023). Teacher Self Care [Video]. Vimeo. https://vimeo.com/601602253/88ba94eb62

The Educator. (2023, May 2). *What drives Australia's school leaders?* https://www.theeducatoronline.com/k12/news/what-drives-australias-school-leaders/282396

Waterford Education. (2023, June 26). *How Family Engagement Leads to Student Success.* https://www.waterford.org/education/how-parent-involvment-leads-to-student-success/

Weldon, P., & Ingvarson, L. (2016). *School Staff Workload Study.* The Australian Council for Educational Research Ltd (ACER). https://research.acer.edu.au/cgi/viewcontent.cgi?article=1028&context=tll_misc

Wells, C. M., & Klocko, B.A. (2018). Principal Wellbeing and Resilience: Mindfulness as a Means to That End. *NASSP Bulletin, 102*(2), 161–173. https://journals.sagepub.com/doi/10.1177/0192636518777813

Wells, C. M., Maxfield, C. R., & Klocko, B. A. (2011). Complexities in the Workload of Principals: Implications for Teacher Leadership. Blazing New Trails: Preparing Leaders to Improve Access and Equity in Today's Schools. In B. J. Alford., G. Perreault., L. Zellner., & J. W. Ballenger (Eds.), *The 2011 Yearbook of the National Council of Professors of Educational Administration* (pp. 29–46). ProActive Publications. https://citeseerx.ist.psu.edu/viewdoc/download?doi=10.1.1.473.3173&rep=rep1&type=pdf#page=43

Wiliam, D. (2017). *Embedded Formative Assessment: Strategies for Classroom Assessment That Drives Student Engagement and Learning* (2nd ed.). Solution Tree Press.

APPENDIX ONE

List of activities that school staff may undertake

- Rescuing baby birds from gutter during school arrival time.
- Protecting nesting curlews outside classrooms.
- Administering first aid while parents fragile with sight of injury.
- Sacking incompetent groundsmen.
- Removing reptiles including snakes, lizards, cane toads and spiders.
- First aid to staff who collapse with a medical condition.
- Take students to police as they are in fear of their parents.
- Take students to visit Dad in jail because Mum can't or won't visit.
- Visit a students' parent in the watch-house.
- Attend funeral of parents.
- Plan funeral for unchurched parents.
- Visit student at home and bring them to school if they are reluctant learners and their parents are incapable of getting them to school.
- Close contract on long serving staff who are dearly loved.
- Counsel staff who are in relationship with divorced parent.
- Facilitating staff who are in conflict, including leadership team members.
- Managing building projects.
- Setting school budgets.
- Managing emotional parent meetings when decisions are out of my hands e.g. funding and staffing.
- Get dressed up and performing for Book Week.
- Sit on dunking machine at school fete (after doing the risk assessment).
- Hold crying babies during enrolment interviews or parent info sessions if babysitting is to be provided.
- Set up for fetes/art shows/trivia nights, close up after the event, late at night or early morning.
- Arrive early to set up for blessing and opening of buildings.
- Host politicians and follow protocols.
- Take students on interstate or overseas trips.
- Negotiate contracts for sponsors or contractors.

- Employ new staff.
- Run assemblies in front of hundreds, possibly thousands of people.
- Make public speech.
- Appear on TV or radio.
- Participate in staff/student sporting games.
- Compete in staff race at carnivals while avoiding injury, and after doing the risk assessment.
- Go on camp and demonstrate activities, which may scare you!!
- Leading church services when priest away (in faith based schools).
- Clean gutters when grounds staff away.
- Substitute for crossing supervisor when away.
- Get in pool late at night to clean out debris after storms.
- Attend to maintenance issue after hours, e.g. broken water pipe, which can't be left overnight.
- Attend to security breaches after hours.
- Assist at church celebrations after hours.
- Lead reviews of school leaders.
- Give constructive feedback to staff.
- Go in ambulance to hospital with staff or students as required.
- Put students in ambulance with sick parent.
- Shave head for worthy cause at school.
- Cleaning vomit at midnight on camp.
- Assisting with toileting of a student with additional needs.
- Negotiating with specialists about the role in schools.
- Armed Services welcoming on ANZAC and Remembrance days.
- Manage evacuation and lockdowns.
- Hosting parents and family of deceased staff members.
- Sing at Christmas concert.
- Perform with staff at P&F trivia night.
- Negotiate with neighbours over water drainage problems or any common issue.
- Negotiate with neighbours about parking limitations especially during school hours/term/fetes.
- Ensuring professional boundaries are kept when staff attend school community social event.

APPENDIX TWO

Amy Green LinkedIn 10/4/22

Why improve Teacher Wellbeing? Because it directly relates to how we work as teachers and how our students learn and grow.

Teacher Wellbeing is not just about who we are as people, it is also very much about how we teach.

When we work on our wellbeing and focus on building resilience, emotional management and positive emotion strategies and also how to maintain and build energy for function and performance, we are inherently impacting how we work as teachers.

Working on these aspects of our wellbeing allows us to better teach, assess learning and work collaboratively and cohesive in teams. We are better able to function throughout the day and develop stronger self-awareness, giving us the self-efficacy needed to continually evolve and adapt as educators.

With this, we are then more able to focus on our teaching and how we work with and contribute to our teams, improving overall collective teacher efficacy. When we achieve this, learning for our students improves.

This is why Teacher wellbeing matters.

APPENDIX THREE

Email folders indicating the numerous 'other' priorities that principals have to juggle

2023

2024

ANZAC Day

APPA/ QCPPA, BACPPA AITSL

ATSI

Board

Catholic Identity project

CENSUS

Charities

Cluster Colleagues   3

Coaching

∨ Compliance
   Annual Plan
   Annual Report
   EIA
   Guardian
   NSSAB Review
   Vision for Learning
   Confidential

∨ Contractors
   Chess
   Coding
   Go Sports

Young Engineers

∨ Curriculum 2022
   ICAS
   ACARA
   Book lists
   PETAA
   Celebration of Learning

∨ Assessment Monitoring tools
   Review and Response
   ATSI

∨ Camps
   Canberra
   BCE support
   Cath Identity
   Choir
   Debating
   EALD
   Enrichment GnT
   Excursions
   Extra Curric

∨ HPE
   Loose Parts play
   Sch Athletics

Incursions

Instru Music

Italian

Library

Music

Planning

RE

∨ Sport
   Zone / District sports
   Reporting
   Resources
   Sustainability
   Young Engineers IN CLASS

∨ Director updates
   Culture Coalition
   Staff Updates
   The Learning Bar   1
   Directors
   Early Years Kindy candK

∨ Enrolments
   Retention
   External review

∨ Finances 2022+

D365

Fees

Promaster

QKR

    Support Accountant

Govt

Health Check

Insurance CCI

Jobs 2022 +

Legals

Listening Survey

∨ Marketing   3

  Media

  Merchandise

  Prep Booklet

  Sch Camera

  Sch Photos

  Signage

  Website

NAPLAN / QCAA

Newsletter

NSSAB

OSHC

Elections

Worlds Teachers Day

Fundraisers

Christmas Carols

RACE DAY

CSPQ

Rewards

Mothers Fathers Day stalls

Fete 2024

Grants

Projects

Walking Bus

Care and Concern

Courses/ Training

Dads lunch

Election

Feast Day

Fete 2022

Golf day

Mothers luncheon

Nude Food

PALS

Socials

∨ Parish

  Servers

  PB4L

  QELi

  Renewal Compliance Guardian

  Renewal Reviews

  Sch Photos

  Sch TV

∨ Self Funded projects

  Awnings Iona

  Awnings Pick up

  Library

  Retention Basin

  Senior Leader BCE

∨ Staff 2022+

  APA   1

  APRE

  ASSURE

  Chaplaincy

  ECT

  Excellence Awards

  Feb floods

  Goal Setting

  Guidance Counsellor

Guidance Counsellor

Health/ family

Learning Enhancement

Level 1

Office Staff

∨ PD Training

  I Learn Course

PLL

QCT

References

Sch Officers

SCIMT

social

Speechy

Staff Mtgs

STIE

∨ Teachers

  HAT / LT / EPT

  Marketplace

  Newsletters

  p/t/ nights

  Prac Students

  Support Team info

  Union hat

  VT HI

VT: PI

Wilston TEAMS

∨ WSS

  Expenses Claims

  Leave appn

  Staff Appts

  Vaccinations

∨ Students

  Tutoring

  Media

  Absentees

  Allied Health Prof

  Awards

  > Behaviour

  COVID

  Disco

  EAP IEPs

  ENGAGE

  Enrichment

  Graduation

  HANSON Bros

  Exiting

  Health Family

  Leadership

  Learning

Mary Mackillop Fund

NCCD

Orientation

Past pupils

PB4L

Prep

references

Repeating or not

Seniors leaders

Student Councillors

Student Protection

Support

> Students w Disability

Transitions

∨ Technology 2022   2

  AV

  Camera

  Committee

  Copier

  Copyright

  Dynamics

  E-Minerva

  FAWMATT

  One to One Program

  Phones

Sch TV
Service desk
teaching resources
Website
Tuckshop   1
U8 Week
Uniform Shop   3
Union
Volunteers
˅ WHS Wilston   1
  Aborist / TRees
  AirCon
  Asbestos
  BCE WHSO
  Classroom
  Classroom inspections
  Cleaners
  Committee
  Contractors
  Drills Evac Ldown
  Electricals
  Emergency lighting
  Facilities Audit 2022
  Fire Safety
  First Aid

Furniture
Groundsmen
LIFT
Maintenance
Neighbours
Painting
Pest servicing
Playgrd
Psychsocial Hazards
Risk Assessment
Road Safety/ Active Sch Tr
SCIMT
Security Keys
Staff Injury / Rehab
Storage off site
Student injuries
Sun Safety
Tennis Courts
Waste Management
WATER Drainage
WHSO
WILSTON
˅ Wilston Building Project
  $$ Claims Insurance
  Blessing and Opening

Tennis Courts
Waste Management
WATER Drainage
WHSO
WILSTON
˅ Wilston Building Project
  $$ Claims Insurance
  Blessing and Opening
  Construction
  Demo
  NBN Telstra Data
  Plans
  Relocation
  Site Mtg Mins
  Tender process
  Wilston Master Plans

Acknowledgements

In writing this book I was conscious to make it relevant for school leaders and aspiring leaders. I sought the wisdom of friends and colleagues in a variety of education sectors. I thank Phillip McGreevy and Alanna Bolger who read the manuscript and gave me some key feedback. I also acknowledge Dr Paul Kidson from Australian Catholic University and Willy Wood from Missouri in the United States, who also took the time to read the manuscript and cast a critical eye over it.

Having someone of the calibre of Dr Michael Stewart read my work and bring his wealth of experience to add to the quality of the content is invaluable. I thank Michael for his time and thoughts.

My career in education has spanned over 35 years. In this time I have worked with many teachers, teacher aides, colleagues and educational leaders. Every interaction, especially in the last few years, has allowed me to reflect on the work and the outcomes. I say thank you to my colleagues who have inspired me, who have shared stories and who have added to my professional journey. The conversations we have had, have brought a depth of reflections to my experiences, some of which are recalled in this text.

I thank my family, Lisa, Zac and Bridget, for their patience when writing absorbed my mind and time. Their words of support are appreciated.

Finally, I thank Alicia Cohen, my trusted publisher, for her words of advice, encouragement and wisdom. Her faith in my writing kept me going when it became 'too hard' on some occasions.

I hope this book adds to the dialogue around the model of education that can provide high-quality teaching and learning for all children, while being life-giving to educators. All educators have to juggle the myriad of responsibilities that exist in schools. We also have a personal responsibility to look after ourselves, while remaining true to our core business, meeting our legal and ethical obligations, while building positive relationships with those with whom we work and educate. If educators don't look after themselves, they cannot educate the students in their care. This book gives the reader some practical tips while juggling our core business and the reality of school life.

I welcome your feedback so we may learn together.

About the Author

Andrew Oberthur has been a teacher for over thirty years and a primary school principal for more than twenty of these. He is a popular speaker, presenter, and facilitator of workshops on creating a culture of trust, collaboration and enquiry between teachers and parents.

Andrew's previous books include:

- *Are You Ready for School?: Trust, Collaboration and Enquiry Between Parents and Teachers* (Amba Press, 2021)
- *Balance: Building Positive Relationships within Educational Protocols* (Amba Press, 2022)

Milton Keynes UK
Ingram Content Group UK Ltd.
UKHW052258160224
437951UK00006B/488